PENGU[...]

BIKE AMBU[...]

Biswajit Jha is a journalist turned social entrepreneur, columnist and author. Jha started his career with the *Pioneer* in 2005 after completing his masters in mass communication.

He was principal correspondent at Zee News and head of the sports department at ZeeNews.com when he decided to quit in 2013, after working in New Delhi for almost nine years, to lead a life of happiness and fulfilment in his village, Rajganj, in West Bengal's Jalpaiguri district. With a guiding principle of doing something for others and uplifting unprivileged children, Jha, along with his wife, Dr Sanjukta Saha, started an educational trust that also runs a school—Epic Public School—in Cooch Behar.

Having identified how hard unemployment hurts the educated youth, Jha advocates social entrepreneurship as the solution. Determined to give back to his roots, Jha took up the responsibility of running the Rajganj Football Academy, which changed the fortunes of many children in his village. A sports buff and fitness freak, he aims to promote stress-free learning through games and yoga.

An adjunct professor of media communication at the Gyalpozhing College of Information Technology in eastern Bhutan's Mongar, Jha is also the joint secretary of the Bengal chapter of the Kudo International Federation of India (KIFI), which is promoted by Bollywood star Akshay Kumar. Jha regularly writes columns for the news portals of national media houses like Times Now, Zee Media, CNN-News18, etc. True to his versatile personality, in 2019, Jha went to China to conduct the Durga Puja for the Bengali community in Beijing. He currently lives with his parents, father-in-law, wife and son in north Bengal.

For more about him, you can visit the links below:
Website: www.biswajitjha.com
Facebook: https://www.facebook.com/biswajit.jha.5
Twitter: @biswajit_jha
Email: biswajitjha013@gmail.com

BIKE AMBULANCE DADA

The Inspiring Story of

KARIMUL HAK

The Man Who Saved over 4000 Lives

BISWAJIT JHA

PENGUIN BOOKS

An imprint of Penguin Random House

PENGUIN BOOKS

USA | Canada | UK | Ireland | Australia
New Zealand | India | South Africa | China

Penguin Books is part of the Penguin Random House group of companies
whose addresses can be found at global.penguinrandomhouse.com

Published by Penguin Random House India Pvt. Ltd
7th Floor, Infinity Tower C, DLF Cyber City,
Gurgaon 122 002, Haryana, India

Penguin
Random House
India

First published in Penguin Books by Penguin Random House India 2021

Copyright © Biswajit Jha 2021

ISBN 9780143449829

Typeset in Adobe Garamond Pro by Manipal Technologies Limited, Manipal
Printed at Thomson Press India Ltd, New Delhi

www.penguin.co.in

MIX
Paper
FSC FSC™ C010615

This book is dedicated to all those people who dare to dream big despite hardships and limitations

Contents

Contents

Preface: Words from Karimul[1]

Let me tell you at the outset that I don't consider myself worthy of all the awards and accolades I have received. I am a simple person with simple desires. Like every son in this world, I loved my mother a lot. As a child, her happiness made me joyful, her sorrow made me sad. So, when she died at home without getting medical treatment because I could not manage an ambulance, I was shattered. I took a pledge that day that I would not allow this to happen to anybody else.

I am a tea garden worker who earns a measly income. I know my limitations; I have neither education nor money. Who would listen to me? But I needed to keep my promise to my dying mother.

---

[1] From an interview dated 2 April 2019 at Karimul's house in Dhalabari, Rajadanga.

I started carrying sick patients to the hospital, first on my bicycle, and later on my motorbike, which I bought with the help of some people.

Apart from that, I have been running a clinic at my home and providing basic healthcare facilities to the poor in my area. I have never done any work thinking that I would be awarded or rewarded. But gradually, people came to know about my free bike ambulance service. Various newspapers and TV channels did some stories on me. Several documentaries were also made on my life. Finally, the central government decided to award me the Padma Shri in 2017.

The award has, in a way, increased my responsibilities, and my sphere of work has expanded manifold. Pursuant to the award, people from diverse backgrounds offered me assistance, so I decided to work on problems in other fields too: education, employment generation and the quality of water in rural areas. I have started working for the differently abled as well.

I am thankful to Biswajit Jha, who has written my official biography, because he knows me personally and is himself associated with social work. He was a journalist in Delhi who quit his job to work for the poor people of north Bengal. I am glad that such a person has documented the story of my life.

I am also happy that it has been written in English as many people outside the periphery of Bengal, and even

India, will be able to read this book. I will be very happy if people, especially the younger generation, are inspired by the story of my life and start working for the society and country.

Introduction

Helping your fellow men were one's only excuse for being in this world, and in the doing of things to help one's fellows lay the secret of lasting happiness.

—Helen Keller[1]

That this book would be written one day was actually decided twenty years ago. It was a sultry summer noon in the early nineties. Hungry and exhausted, an old sanyasi came to our doorstep. My father ushered him into the puja room. After my mother fed him, the sanyasi expressed his wish to rest inside the puja room. But the room did

---

[1] Jessica Koser, 'From the Files: New Library Is Now Open to the Public', *Dunn County News*, 19 January 2016.

not have a ceiling fan as we couldn't afford one in every room. Realizing the old man might not feel comfortable without a fan, my father got the ceiling fan uninstalled from his own room and fixed inside the puja room so that the sanyasi could sleep well.

So, the lesson about doing things for others and sacrificing your own comfort for someone less fortunate than you, I got from my father who, despite being not very well-off, did everything he could his entire life for the betterment of society. He took on a frontal role in establishing three charitable schools in our village and also worked tirelessly to improve education in and around our village. I did not have to go outside my own home to find inspiration to help others.

It is therefore not surprising that my first book should be about 'Bike Ambulance Dada' Karimul Hak who has spent his life serving others, ferrying more than 4000 people to hospitals on his bike. This book's aim is to communicate that miracles happen when you do good to others.

For me, writing a book was a dream—and writing this book was definitely not easy. Not because I can't write, but because of the enormity of the task itself. Taking out time from my busy schedule to write so many pages was a big challenge. As a journalist working in the national media before becoming a social entrepreneur in 2013,

I had written several articles and blogs, but writing a book was a different ball game altogether.

With the agreement to write the official biography of Karimul Hak signed in November 2017, I had to start at some point. My debut book, about the life and journey of Hak, a tea garden labourer, was becoming a reality.

For those not in the know, Karimul Hak was awarded the Padma Shri, the fourth-highest civilian award in India, in 2017 for his free bike ambulance service in the remote areas of West Bengal's Jalpaiguri district.

I began by talking to him, his family members, his close associates, his fellow villagers and other people who knew him well. I also read many newspaper reports about his work and him in the last ten years. It was only in September 2018, finally satisfied with my research on Karimul, that I started writing about the man whom I consider a living legend.

While I had known him well before he received the Padma Shri, it was a tremendous experience getting to know him even more closely. To be in close contact with a man like him is an honour and a privilege. Working with him was a huge joy and an equally great learning experience. Talking to him and watching him was enriching. You are sure to be moved by this great man when you listen to his stories of serving the poor, his vision and his secular nature.

Despite receiving the Padma Shri and signing an agreement for a mainstream biopic, Karimul remains a very down-to-earth person. Although he receives many invitations these days, he doesn't allow them to interfere with his passion for serving the poor.

Hak's life is living proof that you don't have to be an extraordinary person to do extraordinary work. You can be ordinary and still do outstanding work for people. His life is an inspiration for all of us. When a tea garden labourer with a meagre monthly salary can undertake such a path-breaking journey, what is it that holds us back?

1

Padma Who?

Man gives you the award, but God gives you the reward.

—Denzel Washington[1]

It was 23 January 2017. Karimul Hak was very upset.

Dr Khiten Barman, who worked as a medical officer at Uttar Saripakuri Rural Health Centre in Kranti, a friend, philosopher and guiding force in Karimul's spirited and selfless journey to serve the countless poor, was fighting for his life. He had been admitted to Jalpaiguri Sadar Hospital after his car met with an accident. The news reached Karimul around 11 a.m. As he was getting ready to go to

---

[1] https://www.brainyquote.com/quotes/denzel_washington_452366, accessed on 17 December 2019.

Jalpaiguri to be with his guru, Karimul got a call on his cell phone. He was not in the mood to talk to anyone, but he took the call, his sense of commitment compelling him to do so.

A man spoke in Hindi. '*Aap Jalpaiguri ke Bike Ambulance Dada hain?*' (Are you the Bike Ambulance Dada from Jalpaiguri?)

When Karimul replied in the affirmative, the man said, '*Badhai ho, aapko Padma Shri milne waala hai!*' (Congratulations! You have been selected for the Padma Shri).

Oriented to dealing with calls for the bike ambulance service he ran, Karimul asked him, 'What has happened to Padma?' How was the caller related to Padma, he wondered.

The man, who was calling from Rashtrapati Bhavan in New Delhi, then told him about the Padma Shri. Now thinking that some medical issue had befallen famous Bollywood actress Sridevi, Karimul asked the caller what had happened to her!

When the man started to explain, Karimul interrupted him with, 'Just bring the girl to me and I will manage her treatment,' before disconnecting the call, not interested in continuing the conversation, perturbed as he was by the news of Dr Barman's accident.

In no time, Karimul was besieged with phone calls from journalists in West Bengal, informing and congratulating him about being chosen for the prestigious Padma Shri.

Karimul was perplexed: his knowledge of such awards was limited, and consequently he had no idea of its importance. One journalist asked him to tune in to the news channel, which was announcing the names for the civilian awards of 2017. He turned on the TV and was surprised to see his name on national news channels. Finally, he understood that he was going to receive an esteemed award. He had won some awards before, but those had not attracted so much media attention. He became very emotional. Tears started rolling down his face and he remembered his mother's face. That moment made him revisit his mother's agony at the time of her death.

He called out to his wife and sons to come and see the news; they were ecstatic that his life's work had been appreciated and recognized. Anjuwara, his wife, who had been a constant support in his mission to serve people for almost twenty years, could not hold back her tears of joy. As the news spread in his hamlet of Dhalabari, locals gathered at his house, proud and happy for their Karimul. He could not extricate himself from his cell phone, as journalists, relatives and well-wishers kept calling him, commending him, lauding him.

Local journalists started coming in droves: this would be the headline of their newspapers the next day. Reporters of local news channels, as well as national channels, turned up at Karimul's doorstep to interview him. The ramshackle house amid a tea garden was jam-packed with visitors, and most of those who had gathered had no option but to stand, for the small house did not have arrangements for so many people. The Haks, who had been living here for years, had never seen so many people in their home at the same time, not even during any wedding in the family.

Well-placed government officials, too, called up Karimul, applauding him and wishing him the best for the future. The hero of the moment, Karimul, did not know how to respond to so much appreciation and adulation, not only because he had never faced this kind of public attention before, but also because so many of the people who spoke to him were strangers. He was in a daze, barely able to fathom what was happening—but yes, he could sense the excitement, with him at the centre of the hubbub. In a life beset with struggles and tragedies, Karimul was not accustomed to such euphoria.

Karimul had barely had a free moment since receiving the news of Dr Barman's accident. The continuous coming and going of people congratulating him, phone calls and interviews with newspapers, news agencies and news channels, had kept him busy all day. And in between all this, he got the news that Dr Barman had died; his dead body would be brought to Kranti where he had lived his entire life. He was to be cremated there.

Even as waves of joy and cheer surged around him, Karimul was shattered within. He couldn't believe that Dr Barman had left the world on a day when the government had announced his name for such a prestigious award. He couldn't believe that Dr Barman, who had stood beside him like a pillar in his mission of carrying the sick to the hospital on his bike ambulance, was no more. He couldn't believe that the kind soul who had been his support was no more, that the man who deserved a share of credit for Karimul's accomplishments would never know that he had been recognized by the Government of India with the Padma Shri.

He missed the doctor even more as he was surrounded by people: hundreds were thronging to his house to celebrate his success, and numerous others were wishing him over the phone. At a time when very few people had supported his work, Dr Barman had stood by him like a rock. And now, on Karimul's big day, Dr Barman was no more. Could anything be more ironical?

Once Karimul realized his phone wouldn't stop ringing, he handed it over to Raju, his elder son, and headed to Dr Barman's house. When Dr Barman's body reached the house, Karimul dissolved into tears. Karimul longed to wake him up and tell him about the Padma Shri, an award that belonged to Dr Barman as much as to him.

Heart-broken, Karimul silently watched Dr Barman's cremation. He was the last person to leave the crematorium. Raju came around 10 p.m. and took Karimul home. As he sat down for dinner, Karimul, who had gone to bed hungry countless times, realized that food could, sometimes, be tasteless.

The next day passed more or less in the same way, with people pouring in, and more interviews and phone calls. Karimul had received some awards earlier, including the Ananya Samman from news channel Zee 24 Ghanta, in recognition of his extraordinary contribution to society. But the Padma Shri was huge for the people of north Bengal, which is often regarded as a backward area of West Bengal. Karimul was still in shock. Raju gathered all the newspapers that morning and placed them before him. Karimul receiving the Padma Shri was the headline in all the newspapers, with some of them also highlighting the sad demise of his mentor, Dr Barman, on the same day.

After a few days, S.S. Ahluwalia, the then union minister and member of Parliament (MP) from the Darjeeling constituency, visited Karimul at his house. Ahluwalia told him he had come to meet him on the advice of Prime Minister Narendra Modi, who had also congratulated him on being selected for the Padma Shri.

Ahluwalia said this award would give Karimul, so far an unsung hero, a new identity. Karimul had, he said, made history as he had developed a new concept: the novel idea of using a bike as an ambulance. He told the media that Karimul had shown the world that an indomitable spirit could achieve anything.

During his visit, Ahluwalia called up Rahul Bajaj, whose company Bajaj Auto Limited had presented Karimul a specially designed bike ambulance. When Ahluwalia passed the phone to Karimul, Bajaj warmly congratulated him too.

Karimul confessed to the minister that he did not know what the Padma Shri was all about. Serving the sick and needy held more significance for him than the Padma Shri, the humble Karimul told the minister. When the minister asked him what he would like from the government, Karimul requested that the local health centre be upgraded and a bridge be built over the river Chell, which would help around three lakh people.

Felicitations started pouring in. On 26 January 2017, Karimul was specially honoured by the Sub Divisional Officer (SDO) of Malbazar, Jyotirmoy Tanti, during the government's official Republic Day celebrations. Different social organizations, clubs and NGOs called him to hail his efforts. Karimul had suddenly become a superstar. Gradually, he realized that if he attended every felicitation ceremony, his bike ambulance service would suffer. The felicitations were hampering his primary work. During one such programme in Siliguri, Karimul even appealed to everyone not to arrange any more felicitation events but to come forward and help him in his mission.

But people wanted him to attend more and more programmes related to social causes, hoping that his presence and appeal would attract more towards those particular issues. How could he avoid such events? Sometimes, in the middle of a felicitation programme, he would get a call from a relative of a sick person requesting his bike ambulance service. But he would have to say no. Realizing that the Padma Shri was hampering his bike ambulance service, he appointed his two sons to carry on with it.

However, Karimul soon realized that instead of letting his new-found fame obstruct his work, he could utilize it to serve people better, and in diverse ways. Many people from India and abroad had contacted him, offering their help and support, so he now had the option of expanding his area of work.

Now that Karimul knew about and had come to terms with the Padma Shri and its significance, he was confronted with another dilemma. He had no clue where he had to go, and how, to receive this award. The SDO informed him through the Block Development Officer (BDO) that they would purchase a ticket for him to attend the award ceremony at Rashtrapati Bhavan on 30 March. They advised him to reach Delhi on 28 March, as he had to compulsorily attend the dress rehearsal on 29 March.

The local administration organized plane tickets for him and a friend. On 28 March, Karimul boarded a plane for the first time in his life. Excited as he was, Karimul remembered Dr Barman; had the good doctor been alive, he would surely have accompanied Karimul.

When Karimul and his friend landed at the New Delhi airport, they found a car waiting for them, which took them to a famous hotel, The Ashok. Never having entered such a grand hotel before, Karimul had no knowledge of the etiquettes that he needed to display. He only knew how to take critically ill patients to hospitals.

At the dress rehearsal on 29 March 2017, a day before the award ceremony, the recipients were explained the etiquette and protocol they would have to follow while receiving the award from the President. Finally came the red-letter day. Karimul woke up early. He was considerably nervous before meeting the President and prime minister—it was something he had never ever imagined.

All the awardees were taken to Rashtrapati Bhavan, the grandeur of which filled Karimul with awe. In the hall, where the award was to be given, he saw the then

President Pranab Mukherjee, Prime Minister Modi, former deputy prime minister Lal Krishna Advani, and other dignitaries.

When his name was announced for the award, Karimul remembered his mother, whose death had acted as the catalyst for his free bike ambulance service. It was a proud moment for Karimul when he received the award formally from the President.

After the ceremony was over, the awardees and dignitaries were enjoying tea when, suddenly, Prime Minister Modi called Karimul over and embraced him. He congratulated Karimul for his work and exchanged pleasantries with him.

The next day, Karimul visited India Gate, Qutab Minar and several other places he had only heard of. On his way home, Karimul felt a sense of fulfilment and a kind of amazement. Sitting on the return flight, he still couldn't believe what had happened to his life in just a few months. From a tea garden labourer to a Padma Shri awardee! He couldn't believe he had just received such a prestigious award from the President, couldn't believe that Prime Minister Modi had recognized him.

It had been a tremendous journey, one that testified to his indomitable spirit. He thought of all that had transpired in his life so far, all the struggles he had overcome. As he reminisced, tears rolled down his cheeks.

He felt as though he was witnessing a movie based on someone else's life.

Are successful people born or made? Karimul Hak was not born to be successful . . .

2

Born with Hunger

*Life is 10 per cent what happens to me and 90 per cent how
I react to it.*

—Charles R. Swindoll[1]

On 7 June 1965, Karimul was born to Nalua Mohammed
and Jafarunnesa in Dhalabari of Rajadanga, near Kranti
Bazaar, which came under Mal block of West Bengal's
Jalpaiguri district. He was the third child in a family
struggling to make ends meet. Nalua, an honest man,
worked as a night guard for the local zamindar, Kausar
Alam. Jafarunnesa had come from Bangladesh as a

---

[1] https://www.goodreads.com/author/quotes/5139.Charles_R_
Swindoll, accessed on 17 December 2019.

maidservant of Kausar Alam's wife; she worked in the zamindar's house. The zamindar and his family were the most influential people in the area, with a large plot of land. At a time when BMW, Audi and Mercedes-Benz were yet to capture the imagination of the rich and powerful, the elephant served as a status symbol. The zamindar had four.

Along with other villagers, Karimul and his three siblings would watch in fascination when the zamindar and his family, seated on an elephant, would go around the village. Owning an elephant was never the Hak family's dream, far from it. Their only dream was to have something to eat every day—something their father could not provide. Nalua's meagre salary was not enough to support his family. Feeding four children was a challenge, and Karimul faced abject hunger from the day he was born. While there was sibling rivalry, it was only for food. When you are hungry, you can hardly think or feel anything else; the only thing you look forward to is having a meal twice a day.

There were times when the family would sleep on an empty stomach, and with no assurance of food the next day as well. There were times when they went without a proper meal for a week. At such times, they would survive on boiled green banana or boiled jackfruit. Rice, wheat or flour was a distant dream.

Sometimes his mother would bring home some food from the zamindar's kitchen. Karimul and his siblings looked forward to days like that. An air of joy and celebration would envelop their home the day that would happen, but that excitement would soon turn into chaos as the youngsters would try to grab what they could. Poverty and hunger sometimes make you forget everything else. One day, during an altercation with his siblings over lunch, little Karimul hit his father on the forehead with a stick. To this day, he regrets the incident, but it is an indicator of their wretched poverty.

The four children and their parents lived in a dilapidated thatched hut. During winter, they would shiver in the bitter cold and make their bed with paddy straw, which gave them some comfort. And in spite of layering themselves with all the hand-me-downs given to them by better-off villagers, they got little protection from the harsh cold. Karimul still remembers how his soft-spoken mother never got to wear a piece of warm clothing during the winter.

Life was not easy for the Hak family in the rainy season either. Rain would trickle in through the thatched roof and the entire family would spend sleepless nights. Since they did not have enough clothes to change into when they got drenched, they had to spend days in the same wet clothes. It was also difficult to cook in this season as the fuelwood would get wet, making it tough to get the fire going. Karimul would see his mother struggle to light the *chullah*, gusts of smoke making her eyes water.

For her, like all mothers, the well-being of her children was priority. Even now, he gets teary-eyed when he remembers his mother's sacrifices. When he and his siblings quarrelled over the measly helpings of food, his mother would try to pacify them, selflessly giving them her share. He understood much later that his mother had, on many days, gone to bed without eating anything. But such is a mother's love that her children's happiness makes her forget all physical pain, all hunger, all agony.

From a very young age, Karimul was quite attached to his mother and very sympathetic towards her. His father, who was very short-tempered, would shout at his mother every now and then, and Karimul would burst into tears, feeling helpless. Sometimes, Karimul would go and hug his mother, thinking that she was in pain. And she was in pain—fearing that if she didn't manage to make ends meet, her children would starve. But Karimul's hug would comfort her. This bond with his mother remained till her death.

Karimul recalls one evening when he and his mother were on their way home with some rice from Kausar Alam's house. It was an extremely stormy day, with lightning and fierce winds. His mother held the bowl of rice close to her chest; it felt as though if it fell from her hands, they would lose everything. That bowl of rice seemed more valuable than their own lives. When they finally made it home, he felt as though he had escaped from the jaws of death.

Eid was a time that heaped more torment on them. They hardly had to think about fasting during the holy month as they almost observed a fast throughout the year! The day of Eid—which most of Karimul's friends celebrated with fervour—eating delicacies and sporting new clothes—was for him and his siblings like any other day. They spent that day, too, in their old clothes, cursing their fate.

He still remembers his mother's agonized face at being unable to give her children anything during the festival. Even as the children clamoured for goodies and new clothes that they saw their friends enjoying, their mother would remain quiet; she had no words with which to console the little ones.

Those far-from-festive days of Eid in the Hak household left such a mark on Karimul that once he started earning, he began buying clothes for his mother for the festival. Now, in addition to donating old clothes to the poor women of the area, he gives them new clothes for Eid as well. Their blessings ease the pain of the missed Eid days of his childhood.

We truly get to know people in our bad times. Good times seldom teach you anything in life. The closest of relatives choose to look through you, ignoring you in your toughest times. One day, Karimul and his family had gone to a relative's house in their locality. On seeing them arrive, the relative's family hid all the food. The Haks, however, were accustomed to such behaviour.

But not everyone was unkind. There were Good Samaritans too who did what they could. Karimul's friend Khalek was one such. Many a time, Khalek would smuggle rice or flour from his house and give it to Karimul's mother, so that they could eat a proper meal. And because of good souls like Khalek, their humanity, Karimul's family survived.

Though short-tempered, Nalua, Karimul's father, was a noble soul. Despite his own troubles in running his family, he was an uncompromising man. Bengal was going through a political transition during the 1960s. A sense of unrest ran deep in the minds of the poor, and the left parties were uniting the poor and turning them against the zamindars and the rich. Influenced by the left ideology, Nalua joined the anti-Congress movement and became a member of a socialist party, which angered Kausar Alam, a traditional Congressman.

To add to this, Nalua did something which ensured his exit from Alam's employ. One night, during Nalua's duty hours, a thief entered the premises. Nalua's temper got the better of him, and in a fit of rage, he beat the thief to death. These factors eventually led to Nalua being let go, and the beginning of one of the harshest phases of the family's life.

After Karimul's father lost his job, the situation at home became grimmer. Occasionally, Karimul, along with his older brother Khalilur, would catch small fish from the nearby pond and barter these for some flour or rice. The family had to face severe hardships for four or five years before Nalua got a job in the Block Land Revenue Office as a peon.

Karimul remembers being in need of a pair of trousers and eventually getting an old pair from someone. The seat of the trousers was so torn that the neighbourhood boys taunted Karimul saying he had two back lights. Sometimes, Karimul would wear a full-sleeve T-shirt as trousers, the sleeves forming the legs of the trousers.

Despite Nalua's meagre income, he made sure the two boys received basic education. Karimul and Khalilur went to the local primary school, but Karimul was not serious about his studies. He was more interested in playing or going for *palagaan*—a genre of Bengali folk songs or local musical show—or taking part in mock stick-fighting during Muharram.

This irritated Khalilur immensely. He was frustrated with Karimul's attitude towards education and life.

One day, when he got fed up of Karimul's lackadaisical attitude, he beat him up badly. Hurting and in pain, Karimul thought of running away.

But how can one run away from one's destiny?

3

Life in Bangladesh

We learn, grow and become compassionate and generous as much through exile as homecoming, as much through loss as gain, as much as through giving things away as in receiving what we believe to be our due.

—David Whyte[1]

It was 1970. East Pakistan, now called Bangladesh, was in the throes of political turmoil, which eventually led to a war with West Pakistan, now called Pakistan. It was a war in which the Bangladeshis fought for their language, their culture and their literature. Formally called the

---

[1] https://www.brainyquote.com/quotes/david_whyte_707614, accessed on 17 December 2019.

Bangladesh Liberation War, it was popularly known as *muktijuddho*.

Pre-independence unrest in the Indian subcontinent had seen millions of people being massacred in one of the worst bloodbaths, after which India and Pakistan attained freedom in August 1947. However, the problems of this region were far from over. Pakistan was carved out in the name of religion. Generally, with some exceptions, Muslim-dominated areas were included in Pakistan, whereas Hindu-dominated areas became a part of India.

Thus, two countries were created, India and Pakistan, with the latter comprising two parts, a western part (West Pakistan) and an eastern part (East Pakistan). India geographically separated these two parts. Still, with Islam as the common uniting factor, the two parts remained one nation despite several—political, cultural, linguistic and ideological—differences.

What the West Pakistani leaders did not realize was that sometimes language and culture can overpower religious sentiments. With the passage of time, the differences widened; the resentment intensified to such an extent that apart from a few fundamental Islamists and Urdu-speaking Biharis, most of the Bengali-speaking Muslim majority clamoured for its own country and freedom from Pakistani rule.

In 1971, the Pakistani army launched Operation Searchlight[2] in which millions of East Pakistanis were brutally killed, women raped and many people rendered homeless, some fleeing to India. When minority Hindus were separately targeted by the army, millions of Hindus had no option but to seek shelter in India.

Karimul's mama (mother's brother) Ashraful, who was a daily wage labourer in Bangladesh's Barakhata village, joined this war. One night, when Ashraful was in bed, some Pakistani army jawans came searching for him. He managed to escape and walked the whole night to cross the border into India. Two days later, he reached his elder sister's place in Rajadanga village.

Karimul's family was happy to see Ashraful. But Ashraful was in deep agony, having left his wife and children behind. He had no idea whether they were alive or had been killed by the Pakistani army. In exile, he found solace in Karimul's fun-loving company. The nephew–uncle duo got along well, often attending several cultural programmes together, including palagaan at night.

Back home, East Pakistan, with the active support of India, won the thirteen-day-long military war with West Pakistan. On 26 March 1971, East Pakistan finally

---

got its independence and a new nation, Bangladesh, was created. Ashraful, like so many Bangladeshis, was elated. Away from his motherland, he celebrated the creation of Bangladesh, a place where their own language and culture would be celebrated and they would not be treated as inferiors. Filled with joy, he began to prepare for his journey back to Bangladesh, to the wife and children he had left behind.

This was a few days after Karimul was thrashed by his elder brother for not studying, after which he had wanted to run away. Seeing that Ashraful was leaving for Bangladesh, Karimul followed him to the bus stop. Ashraful espied him and asked him to return home. But Karimul was adamant. When the bus arrived, Karimul also boarded the bus and Ashraful was forced to take him to Bangladesh.

Those days communication was not easy. When Karimul did not return home that evening, his family grew worried. There was no sign of him the next day as well. His parents and sisters were shocked that Karimul had run away from home. Khalilur was especially devastated as he realized that the beating he had doled out to Karimul had led to this. Everybody in the family blamed him for the predicament.

Just when the family was beginning to think they had lost Karimul forever, they received a telegram. It was from Ashraful. Karimul had insisted on coming with him to

Bangladesh and was with him. The family could finally breathe easy.

However, after the devastating genocide, life in Bangladesh was tough. Moreover, a cyclone had struck the country, which added to the woes of the people. It is believed the cyclone killed almost three to five lakh people, while the liberation war claimed around thirty lakh lives.

There was complete chaos in the newly formed country that Karimul landed in. He saw severed heads lying around, emaciated people who looked close to death. These were shocking sights, especially for a six-year-old. Suddenly, his own problems looked insignificant when compared to those of the people here.

When he and Ashraful reached home, Karimul's mami (his uncle's wife), Nina Begum, and his cousins were delighted to see Ashraful safe and sound. It was a happy reunion for the family of eight: the couple and their three sons and three daughters. But soon the joy turned a little sour when they realized Karimul would be staying with them. Nina had had a tough time bringing up six children all by herself, working in a few households to keep the family alive without her husband. Now, there was another mouth to feed.

Seeing this could lead to trouble at home, Ashraful approached Ariful Islam, a rich man in Barakhata, requesting him to keep Karimul with his family. He readily accepted the offer. Karimul stayed with Ariful's family for the next ten years, assisting them in different household chores. Around the same time, he was admitted to Class I in the local primary school. Never interested in studies, Karimul struggled at school. When he failed in Class III, he quit school at the age of ten.

Meanwhile, Karimul's absence was of course making his mother very unhappy. She wept for days and kept asking Nalua and Khalilur to go to Bangladesh and bring Karimul back. But the adamant Nalua refused to do so as he was very upset with Karimul for abandoning his family. He declared they would not bring him back.

At Ariful Islam's house, Karimul had a comparatively better life. He was a cheerful child, so everyone in the family liked him, treating him with affection. The Islams had two houses; apart from the house in Barakhata village, there was one in Rangpur town. Since they owned land in Barakhata, they would stay there during the sowing and harvesting seasons. At other times, mostly on weekends, they would visit Rangpur after taking an overnight train.

Once, they visited Dhaka for the medical treatment of Ariful Islam's elder brother. This was Karimul's first visit to a big city. In between medical check-ups, they visited several places in Dhaka. And this was when Karimul saw and boarded a steamer for the first time. It was a memorable experience for him. Sitting in the steamer, he suddenly thought of his mother; he wanted his mother to have this wonderful experience too. He wished he could go back, but the thought of his father and elder brother scared him. He was ready to spend his life in exile rather than face them.

Karimul's trip to Dhaka was a pleasant one, but one incident cast a pall over it. One night, when they were having dinner at an eatery, a beggar suddenly came and snatched his plate. After the war and cyclone, the economic situation in Bangladesh was in tatters. Lakhs of Bangladeshis had turned beggars. The young Karimul was very affected by the sight of so many starving people. Occasionally, he would save rice from his lunch and feed some beggars. But he often felt frustrated that he couldn't do more.

Soon after independence, Bangladesh also saw a devastating spread of cholera, which claimed more lives. Sometimes, villagers would beat empty oil drums at night, hoping to ward off the 'ghost' of cholera. Karimul saw tremendous suffering during his stay in Bangladesh. The nation had got its independence through a hard-fought battle, the effects of which could be seen in every sphere of life. Yet, it continued to face many more challenges.

Amidst these distressing conditions, Karimul had some enjoyable times as well. It was around 1975 that he and

Ariful Islam visited Hussain Muhammad Ershad, who later became the President of Bangladesh.

Ershad was the pride of Rangpur district, and at that time deputy chief of army staff. He was originally from Dinhata of Cooch Behar province (which later merged with India and is now a district under West Bengal) in undivided India. He crossed the border after 1947 and settled in East Pakistan's (now Bangladesh) Rangpur district, which is a neighbouring district of India. Karimul had heard of Ershad and had requested Ariful to take him to meet him. Ariful, who was very fond of Karimul, did not disappoint the lad. Ershad was sitting with his friends on the verandah of his house in Rangpur town. He recognized Ariful and chatted with Karimul as well. When he came to know that Karimul was from India, he shared his childhood stories of Dinhata with him. Karimul was impressed by the simplicity of the man who would later form the Jatiya Party and rule Bangladesh for almost seven years.

Karimul also met noted Bangladeshi actor Tele Samad. Samad had at that time just started his career. He had come to Rangpur to shoot for a film, and that is where Karimul met him. Karimul had always been fond of songs, dance and films. When he heard of Samad's visit to Rangpur, Karimul requested Ariful to take him to see the shooting. After the shoot, they met Samad and a special bond was forged.

As the years passed, a lot changed on the political front. 'Bangabandhu' Sheikh Mujibur Rahman, who had played a pivotal role in Bangladesh's freedom struggle and become its first President, and later prime minister, was assassinated in 1975. It was carried out by some disgruntled elements of his own party, Awami League, who had invaded the presidential house and killed almost every member of his family. Only his daughters, Sheikh Hasina Wazed and Sheikh Rehana, who were out of the country at that time, survived. Hasina later became the president of the Awami League and the prime minister of her country.

Young Karimul, though, was barely aware of the political developments of the country he was living in. The only time he truly had a sense of the political chaos the country was mired in was when the then President, Ziaur Rahman, was assassinated in 1981. Karimul was in Rangpur when the news of the assassination broke out. Violence, in the form of an angry mob, stalked the streets, creating havoc. Houses and shops were set on fire. Karimul took shelter in a house and hid there for two days.

As the turmoil in Bangladesh continued, Karimul grew restless, wanting to return to his motherland, India. Coincidentally, this was when he got a telegram from Khalilur.

4

Tying the Knot

Neither man nor woman is perfect or complete without the other. Thus, no marriage or family, no ward or stake is likely to reach its full potential until husbands and wives, mothers and fathers, men and women work together in unity of purpose, respecting and relying upon each other's strengths.

—Sheri L. Dew[1]

Back home, Nalua was preparing for Khalilur's marriage after he turned twenty. But Khalilur was adamant that he would not get married unless Karimul came back. He loved his brother and the memory of the day when he had beaten

---

[1]   *G's Daily Prayers and Encouragements: Prayer Changes Things*, Calvin C. Gordon.

up Karimul still tormented him. It was 1981; almost ten years since Karimul had left home.

Khalilur sent a telegram to Ashraful in Bangladesh about the plans for his wedding and requested him to send Karimul back home. And fifteen days or so later, Karimul was back from Bangladesh. He was now a young man of sixteen.

In those days, with no Facebook, Instagram or WhatsApp, there was no readily available photograph of a dearly loved one who had been away for a long time. Karimul looked completely different from the little boy who had left home. He was now an adolescent, with a thin moustache and a straggly beard.

Everyone in the family became emotional on seeing Karimul after so many years. His mother could not talk; she kept hugging and kissing him, crying all the while. Both his sisters were crying with joy too, while his father was misty-eyed at seeing his long-lost son, even as he rebuked him for running away. A little away from the others was his elder brother, sitting on the verandah of their house, sobbing. Karimul went up to him and embraced him. Tears flowed freely from their eyes, as the brothers stood in each other's arms, united once again; they did not realize how long they cried like that.

Karimul had always been a music buff. In Bangladesh, Ariful had bought him a tape recorder, a prized possession at that time. Karimul had brought it back with him to his village. This was the first personal music system owned by anyone in Rajadanga; many of the villagers had never seen such a thing before. His family members and the villagers, who had gathered around to catch a glimpse of him, were astonished when he played it. It instantly uplifted everyone's mood, and, surprised and excited, they fell over each other to touch this new object that could produce music so easily.

Karimul would sometimes play some Bangladeshi film music which enthralled and mesmerized the villagers. For the next few months, it was practically the only thing the locals did—play music on the tape recorder to their heart's content. Karimul had also brought with him other treasures such as four pairs of trousers, or full pants as they were then called; Ariful had given him four of his used trousers.

When Karimul had left for Bangladesh years ago, the financial situation at home had been pitiful. His father had been jobless, and going to sleep on an empty stomach was nothing new for the family. Now, after his return from Bangladesh, he was deeply relieved to see that the family's financial health had improved somewhat. His father was working as a peon. Though it was a poorly paid job, it was, nevertheless a government job, and a salary was assured at the end of the month. That his elder brother, too, was working—at a local ration shop—was another blessing.

There was one more reason for Karimul to smile. The family, along with many other villagers, had got some land as landless farmers after the left government came to power in 1977. After assuming office, the Jyoti Basu-led left government soon started a massive land reform project in Bengal, known as Operation Barga. Under this reform, which was started in 1978, sharecroppers or *bargadar*s were given legal rights of the farmlands. The government enlisted the names of sharecroppers in a simple manner so that the uneducated farmers did not have any difficulty in getting their rights registered.

As we have read in history, farmers and tenants were regularly exploited by the landlords, in both old and novel ways. Earlier, most bargadars avoided registering their names and their exploitation would continue under the existing laws. And since they were financially dependent on the landlords, the process of registering was not easy. Additionally, there was this fear, unfounded or otherwise, that if they took the initiative to record their lands, they would be evicted as bargadars.

Apart from registering the names of the bargadars, the government also brought land ceiling into force. The surplus lands of the zamindars and rich villagers were distributed among the landless poor and marginalized sections of the society. Thus, Bengal had undergone a sea change at the grassroots level during the ten years or so that Karimul had been in Bangladesh.

When the left government won the 1977 assembly elections, Karimul's village had also celebrated the party's victory, with other parts of Bengal. His father had once been reviled by the then ruling party leaders and the local zamindar Kausar Alam for joining a left party. Several acres of Kausar's land were now vested and many of the villagers, including Karimul's father, got some share of the land. It was another matter that they could never do any farming for want of funds.

For people like Nalua, who had been exploited by the rich zamindars in different ways, it was a time to be hopeful about their future. They felt their voice would now, finally, be heard.

Even though their house was still a thatched hut, now, thanks to all these developments, the family had a separate room for a kitchen. The family had also decided to construct another room to be used by the elder son after his marriage.

In 1982, Khalilur's marriage was finally arranged with a girl from a nearby village. As Karimul had returned from Bangladesh, Khalilur had no reason to say no to the wedding. Since money was still limited, they could not spend much on the wedding. The marriage took place in a nearby mosque in the presence of family members and close friends.

During the wedding, Karimul's father noticed a girl, who was Khalilur's cousin sister-in-law. He made up his mind that he would get his younger son married to that girl.

One year had passed since Karimul's return from Bangladesh, and during this period he had put in considerable efforts to pick up the threads with his family and childhood friends, and re-establish bonds. It was tough, though; he had spent the last ten years of his life in a completely different place and with completely different people. Not surprisingly, home didn't feel like home any longer. Every now and then, he would miss Rangpur and Barakhata, where he had grown up, as well as Ariful and all his friends and acquaintances back in Bangladesh.

Occasionally, the thought of crossing over to Bangladesh came to his mind. One of Karimul's friends informed Khalilur that Karimul was toying with the idea of going back to Bangladesh. Worried, Khalilur decided that the only way to foil Karimul's plan was to get him married as early as possible.

Khalilur brought up the matter with his father, who told him about Khalilur's cousin sister-in-law. Khalilur liked the girl very much, but he did not like the idea. He told Nalua that he did not want their family to have daughters-in-law from the same family. This infuriated Nalua, who had made up his mind, and he swore that no matter what, he was not going to change his decision. On the other hand, Khalilur also remained adamant and declared he would not allow his brother's marriage with that particular girl.

The person who mattered most in this decision—Karimul—had, in the meantime, developed a soft corner for the girl his father had chosen for him. While all these arguments were going on about selecting a bride for him, he confided to his mother that he liked the girl with whom he had interacted during Khalilur's wedding. However, he did not have the courage to tell Khalilur this; he was afraid of Khalilur whose thrashing had once forced him to flee. Neither did he want to complicate things by admitting his choice.

Meanwhile, Khalilur sought help from some village elders, as well as his relatives, to persuade his father to reconsider his decision. After a lot of hectic parleys, his father finally agreed that two sisters should not be married into the same house as it might create problems later. It was believed that there was more likelihood of misunderstandings or ego clashes among sisters, which could lead to a family feud. But Nalua put forward a condition. He asked Khalilur to find a girl for Karimul and fix the marriage within seven days.

Khalilur now had a serious challenge on hand. He informed everyone he knew of this recent development and urged them to find a suitable bride for Karimul as soon as possible. Sablu Islam, a relative from his in-laws' side, informed Khalilur about his niece who lived in Bokali near Maynaguri (also in Jalpaiguri district). On the fifth day of his father's ultimatum, Khalilur, Sablu and three others visited the girl at her house. They liked her. Considering that he had to meet the deadline set by his father, Khalilur did not waste time and promptly fixed Karimul's marriage with Anjuwara Begum.

Since Khalilur had to hurry things up, he asked four members of his group to go back to the village and bring Karimul with them so that they could get done with the marriage ceremony at the earliest. But back home, his father and Karimul were yet to be convinced about the girl. It took a great deal of effort to convince the father–son duo. The following day, they went to Anjuwara Begum's house for the wedding ceremony. Karimul saw Anjuwara, and though he was not entirely happy with the decision, he agreed to marry her to avoid further tension in the family. Like his father, Karimul, too, had a condition: he would agree to his brother's choice only if they organized a ceremony to celebrate his marriage back home. Khalilur readily agreed to this condition.

They completed the ceremony that day itself in Anjuwara's house and returned to their Rajadanga home, which was about 35 kilometres away. After two days, the family threw a reception party where almost 150 people, including local villagers and their relatives, were invited. Given Karimul's fun-loving nature, he made sure there was music and that everyone sang and danced.

By the time the two brothers got married, their mother had become a little older, and very frail. The two daughters-in-law gradually took over the responsibilities of their mother-in-law who was by now suffering from one ailment or the other. Karimul, by then, had started working as a temporary labourer here and there. But, deep down, he continued to miss Bangladesh and, sometimes, would still think of crossing the border to Bangladesh.

Though Karimul married Anjuwara, he wasn't attracted or attached to his wife. He didn't feel comfortable in the marriage as it had happened against his wish. He hardly stayed at home during the day and often didn't come back at night. His behaviour made Khalilur worry again. After six months of his marriage, Khalilur got the impression that Karimul was planning to run off to Bangladesh. He asked his wife, Kahinoor Begum, to talk to Karimul's wife and warn her that if Karimul went to Bangladesh, Anjuwara would have to accompany him.

Taken aback and not at all keen on taking his wife along with him, Karimul permanently dropped the idea of scampering off to Bangladesh. In the meantime, in 1983, Anjuwara became pregnant with their first child.

5

Lucky No More

You don't choose your family. They are God's gift to you, as you are to them.

—Desmond Tutu[1]

On the day that Anjuwara Begum went into labour, the Hak family prayed for a smooth delivery and a healthy child. Seeing her agony, Karimul wanted to take Anjuwara to the hospital but, in those days, it was almost impossible to take a sick villager to the hospital as there was no vehicle, let alone an ambulance, in their village. Left with no other option, the helpless Karimul could only hope that all would go well. It did; after three or four hours

---

[1] *God Has a Dream: A Vision of Hope for Our Time,* Desmond Tutu.

of pain, Anjuwara gave birth to a beautiful girl at home. Delighted, the family hoped that the baby would bring good fortune to their family. So, they named her Lucky. Unable to contain his happiness, the new father, Karimul, went from door to door in his village, informing the villagers of his daughter's birth.

Lucky truly brought luck for them as, after her birth, Karimul became conscious of his responsibilities and started to work seriously, even though he did not have a permanent job. He would work as a daily wage labourer or as an assistant to truck drivers. Sometimes he worked as a daily wage labourer by the Chell, taking out sand from the bed of the river and loading it in trucks.

On the home front, everyone was glad that Karimul had finally become responsible, taking his new role as a father seriously. Lucky, with her charm, brought joy and cheer into the family. Karimul would come back from work in the evening and play with her. Just six months before Lucky was born, his sister-in-law Kahinoor Begum had given birth to a baby boy. Lucky was the first girl child in this generation and, thus, was special for them. Karimul's family was modern in its outlook compared to their relatives and other villagers. For instance, neither of the brothers had taken dowry from their in-laws. So, it was not surprising that the family welcomed Lucky with joy.

His parents, especially Jafarunnesa, were jubilant at the birth of their two grandchildren; now, after years of struggling, they were able to have some fun with the little ones. But amidst all the happiness, Karimul was deeply concerned about his mother's health, which was going downhill day by day. Sometimes, Karimul would sit with his mother, gently inquiring about her health, chatting with her, encouraging her, doing his utmost to keep her spirits high. She, on the other hand, would do whatever she could to convince her son that she was fine and healthy. Deep down, Jafarunnesa knew she was not well; a continuous ache at the back of her head and a feeling of uneasiness gnawed at her.

As the days flew by, the kids kept the entire household on its toes with their endearing antics. Although both the children were a joy, the family had a softer corner for the pretty and cheerful Lucky. When she was about seven months old, Lucky fell ill, with continuous fever. The doctor at the local health centre was unable to diagnose her malaise. The helpless family called the local witch doctor, but the situation only went from bad to worse. When the little girl did not urinate for two days and became unconscious, Karimul rushed her to Jalpaiguri Sadar Hospital, around 45 kilometres away. She was admitted there for seven days, but the doctors could not save Lucky. She passed away in the hospital.

Grief engulfed the whole family. Karimul was in deep shock. He stopped talking to others and would behave erratically, sometimes bordering on insanity. He stopped going to work, which made things difficult for his family. After around three months of Lucky's death, Karimul became a little stable and resumed work as a daily labourer.

After some months, when his wife conceived again, Karimul settled down, realizing that he would once again become a father. During this period, he did many odd jobs, including working at the nearby Odlabari Tea Estate as a tea plucker. However, it was difficult to get work every day, and the family struggled to manage. Karimul's family was also growing fast. His oldest son, Raju, was born in 1984, followed by Liza after two and a half years; Shimu was born in 1989 and then Rajesh in 1991. By this time, Khalilur's five children were also born. Since they all lived together, the family income was impacted by the addition of so many more members. Jafarunnesa used to take care of all the children at home.

When Jafarunnesa fell ill, both Karimul's wife and sister-in-law had to shoulder all the burden of the care of their small children. As it often happens, after Jafarunnesa fell sick, Nalua married again in 1985. Later, his second wife gave birth to a boy and a girl.

With every passing day, Jafarunnesa was steadily sinking, and around 1989, she suffered a brain stroke that left her paraplegic. Since the two daughters-in-law were fully occupied with their children and other household chores, Karimul and Khalilur would take care of their mother as best as they could, seeing to her needs before leaving for work and after returning home. Karimul continued to work in various places, doing varied jobs. Besides working as a daily wage labourer at Odlabari Tea Estate and tea factories, he also tried his hand at running a paan shop and tea stalls in local fairs which invariably popped up during Durga Puja.

Despite his own hardships, Karimul was always ready to help out any villager. Whenever anyone was in trouble or needed help, Karimul would be there, beside them, supporting them in every way he could. Whether someone had to be taken to the hospital, or needed documents from the panchayat or the block office, he was there to lend a hand. Sometimes, he would take the sick to the hospital on his own, on his bicycle.

In 1987, Karimul himself met with a horrific motorbike accident that left him with a badly broken right leg. He was riding a bike that belonged to the father of Reyaj Chowdhury, the manager of Subarnapur Tea Estate. Karimul was en route to Malbazar with one of his friends riding pillion when the bike suddenly had a flat tyre, because of which he lost balance and the bike landed on his right foot. His friend, who suffered a minor injury, stopped a car and rushed Karimul to a nearby hospital, but they referred him to Jalpaiguri Sadar Hospital. Karimul was confined to the house for six months, which added to his woes. While it may not be immediately obvious, the accident resulted in Karimul walking with a limp: his right leg is slightly bent and shorter than his left leg, and it still gives him trouble while walking.

Karimul continued to be dogged by problems. Around the time Jafarunnesa became severely ill and bedridden, his in-laws too found themselves in a big financial mess after a devastating flood. His aged parents-in-laws' health, too, was becoming a matter of concern. Karimul purchased a plot of land for his in-laws, close to his home. They constructed a thatched house there in 1990, and moved in. Karimul also contributed to their household costs.

While not everyone has shown the kind of gratitude Karimul deserved, there were some good friends who always stood by him in his difficult days, and he is immensely grateful to them for all they did for him and his family. One such person was Tahidul, who sold vegetables in the local Kranti market. Whenever he was left with unsold vegetables, Tahidul would pass them on to Karimul, which was of considerable help. Sometimes, the manager of Subarnapur Tea Estate, Reyaj Choudhury, would also help. He also helped by taking care of the jewellery for Karimul's two daughters when they got married. Another benefactor was Rejaul Karim, a primary teacher at Rajadanga Primary School where Karimul's children studied. He helped Karimul in his own way.

Fighting as he was against many odds, Karimul could not provide his children with basic food, let alone nutritious food. He reared hens at home, so the children could have eggs—but only occasionally, as the family had to sell eggs so that they could buy rice or flour. Likewise, although they had banana trees in their garden, the bananas had to be sold to meet the basic needs of the children.

Karimul's and Khalilur's children went to the local primary school. But because of his financial constraints, Karimul was unable to provide them the support they needed to do well in their studies. The children would often go to school without a copy or a pencil. Besides, since none of the adults in the family had studied much, there was no one to guide or teach the children. And their financial situation made it impossible to arrange tutors for them. The outcome was that not one of Karimul's children was able to complete Class X. To this day, he rues the fact that he could not help his children with their education. In an attempt to salvage the situation, Karimul enrolled his elder son, Raju, in Class X, in open school.

Like others, Karimul was forced to work in far-off Odlabari Tea Estate as there were no tea gardens nearby back then. In 1991, Kailashpur Tea Estate decided to set up Dhalabari Tea Garden in this area. Since the soil was not fertile enough for paddy cultivation, the farmers had decided to sell off their lands to the garden owners. Karimul was keen that a tea garden come up in their area, so that local people could get jobs close by and earn a decent living, which had been impossible so far despite the farmlands they owned.

But the initiative ran into trouble. The local left leadership was against the setting up of tea gardens on farmland. They took out rallies and protest marches. They even gheraoed the tea garden authorities.

By this time, the left, which had come to power fourteen years ago, had established a stronghold in every sphere of life. The party had become bigger than the government and had started taking decisions that, most of the time, were against the interests of the common people. Left-dominated labour unions had become so powerful that they had started calling the shots in tea gardens, factories and other industrial projects in West Bengal. Trade unionism had become militant unionism in Bengal during the left period. Businessmen were seen as class enemies. Whenever there was any dispute, the unions would gherao the managers or owners of the company until they gave in to their demands.

Most of the thriving industries were in trouble due to this militant trade unionism, which resulted either in shutting down of factories or mass exodus of industrialists from West Bengal. The consequent economic decline further aggravated the pathetic unemployment scenario, and the economic situation of Bengal went from bad to worse. Bengal, once the leading state in every sector, started losing its advantage under the left rule.

Karimul's father was a leftist. It was natural that Karimul, too, was inclined towards the left parties. But the Dhalabari incident and the overall radical approach of the left towards industry, even towards agriculture, changed his mind and Karimul grew very disillusioned with their politics. Along with the villagers of Dhalabari, he formed a stiff resistance against the left leaders who finally had to give in. The villagers sold their plots of land and helped set up the Dhalabari Tea Garden, which ensured daily earnings for the poor people of the area.

It was a great achievement, as well as a source of immense satisfaction, for Karimul. After all, making efforts for the villagers had always been his priority.

6

The Making of
Bike Ambulance Dada

*The most beautiful people we have known are those who have
known defeat, known suffering, known struggle, known loss,
and have found their way out of those depths.*

—Elisabeth Kubler-Ross[1]

The two brothers, Karimul and Khalilur, took very good
care of their mother, tending to her needs and adjusting
their daily schedule according to her requirements.
However, Jafarunnesa was getting worse with each passing
day. The situation came to a head on a cold December day
in 1995. Uncomfortable and restless throughout the day,

---

[1] https://www.aquinasacademy-pittsburgh.org/myaquinas/
confidence/parentcommunication5-3-3-14.pdf

the critically ill Jafarunnesa lost consciousness at night. Karimul realized they needed to take her to Jalpaiguri Sadar Hospital immediately.

In those pre-telecom revolution days, only a privileged few had landline phones; the common man using a mobile phone was a distant dream, and it was rare for poor families to have a landline. That's why a frantic Karimul had to rush to Kranti Bazaar, about three kilometres from his home, on that wintry night, to find even a car to take his mother to the hospital. He knew getting hold of an ambulance would be impossible. Karimul sought help from a businessman who had an Ambassador car and was willing to help, but his driver was unavailable that night.

Karimul knew there was little time to waste: if he failed to take his mother to the hospital right away, he would lose her. She had been gasping when he had left home to look for a doctor. He could feel his whole world falling apart in front of him. But there was little he could do.

Faced with this emotionally overwhelming crisis, Karimul was unable to think clearly. All he could do was pray to God to save his mother—or, rather, beseech Allah to send an ambulance. Helpless, Karimul sat on the roadside and broke down, crying his heart out. Then, remembering the pain etched on his mother's face, he dashed home, to his mother's bedside. Holding her hand, Karimul tearfully apologized to his unconscious mother for his inability to take her to the hospital. Soon after, in front of his own eyes, his mother breathed her last.

After that, Karimul became despondent. That his mother had died without proper treatment, that he couldn't take her to the hospital because there was no ambulance in their locality gnawed at him, haunted him.

For many great people, a trigger changes the course of their life, prompting them to think radically and do the impossible, the unthinkable. Jafarunnesa's death was that moment for Karimul, the one that changed his life completely. For the next six months or so, he could not sleep properly, could not talk to anyone properly, and could not eat properly. The circumstances of his mother's death tortured him. He would often have nightmares of his mother dying without treatment, making him relive that moment again and again. Karimul stayed away from work for a few months, brooding day and night.

Eventually, the thought of doing something for the poor, who mostly die because of lack of proper and timely medical attention, or lack of ambulance services, took root in his mind. But he was so beset with problems in his personal life that he pushed the thought away. He did not have any permanent work and was mostly dependent on a daily wage labourer's job, without any guarantee of regular earnings. With his children growing up fast, it was getting more and more difficult for him to provide for his own family.

And then there came a ray of hope. One day, at Kranti Bazaar, he met Reyaj Chowdhury, the manager of Subarnapur Tea Garden and also a relative. Chowdhury asked him to work in his tea garden. Karimul readily joined from the next day as a labourer. After working there for a year, he was made a permanent employee.

One day in 1999, when Karimul was at work, Aijul Haque, a co-worker, collapsed. The workers tried to call an ambulance but were unable to arrange one. Time was running out—Aijul needed immediate medical attention. As Karimul realized that Aijul would die without treatment, the pain of his mother's death revisited him. Suddenly, he had an idea. He grabbed the manager's motorbike and asked a fellow worker to tie Aijul to his back with a piece of cloth. With Aijul riding pillion, Karimul made straight for the nearest local health centre.

When the doctors at the health centre told him to hasten to the district hospital, Karimul rushed immediately, with Aijul still fastened to his back, to the district hospital. Later, when Aijul recovered, the doctors told Karimul that his intervention had saved Aijul's life.

The incident was an eye-opener for Karimul. That a motorbike could do the work of an ambulance and save a life had never occurred to him. The idea of buying a motorbike to take poor patients to hospital now took hold of him, and he became obsessed with this one desire. He thought that if he could do this, his mother would finally find peace in heaven, and his duty towards his mother, which he had failed to perform due to the unavailability of an ambulance, would be fulfilled. At least poor villagers would get timely medical attention.

But setting aside money from a paltry income to buy a motorbike was tough. Still, he did what he could with his limited resources. He started to carry patients to the hospital on his bicycle. Whenever he heard of a poor person in need of medical attention, Karimul would hurry to the patient's home and ferry them to the hospital. If it was not possible to carry the patient to the hospital on his bicycle, he would accompany them.

Meanwhile, pressing matters on the home front took up a considerable portion of his time and energy, leaving him mentally and physically exhausted. His two daughters Liza and Shimu had now reached marriageable age.

One night, when the family was at dinner, Khalilur raised the subject of the marriage of the two girls. Seeing Karimul's indifference to his queries, Khalilur became furious and shouted at him for neglecting his family. Karimul tried to defend himself but, unable to handle Khalilur's wrath, walked out halfway through dinner. Both Karimul's wife and Khalilur's wife tried to pacify

Khalilur, who had always been upset over Karimul's casual approach. Forever busy helping others, Karimul hardly ever gave his own family much thought. And in recent times, Karimul had been caught up with only one thought—how to buy a bike and serve the patients of his area.

Khalilur passed the word among relatives for a suitable boy for Karimul's elder daughter, Liza. Six months passed without a positive response from any of them. Karimul, as usual, remained nonchalant about the issue, but Khalilur kept up the pressure. Finally, Karimul requested his friends and acquaintances to find a groom for Liza. A couple of months later, one of Karimul's friends told them about someone who owned a grocery shop at Paan Bari, around 20 kilometres from Dhalabari.

A date was fixed for a meeting. The prospective groom, his parents and two relatives came to Karimul's house. Karimul, despite his straitened circumstances, arranged lunch for all of them. The visitors chatted with Karimul, Liza and other members of the family. Once the boy's family left, Karimul's family discussed the day's events and came to the same conclusion: that the boy's folks had liked Liza a lot. The Hak family was in a celebratory mood, sensing that the marriage would finally be fixed. The next day, Karimul and Khalilur started making arrangements for Liza's wedding.

As they were getting set for the marriage, a relative from the would-be groom's home came to visit them. Karimul was very happy to see him, but what he heard shocked him. Yes, the groom's side liked the girl very much, but they wanted Rs 20,000 as dowry. Karimul was very upset.

Though he did not utter a single word in front of the man, Karimul decided right away to not go ahead with the wedding, as it would be impossible to arrange the money and, more importantly, on principle, he was against dowry. After the man went away, Karimul discussed the matter with Khalilur who, despite the demand for dowry, was keen on the marriage. Khalilur assured him that he would borrow money from relatives for the purpose, as asking for and giving dowry for a daughter's marriage was a done thing in the village. But Karimul was adamant on calling off the marriage and not giving in to this demand. He regarded dowry as the root cause of domestic violence, inflicted on women who were harassed and even killed in their in-laws' house. Khalilur tried to convince Karimul to decide otherwise, but eventually he had to back off in front of Karimul's stiff resistance. It was decided that they would call off the marriage.

After this incident, Karimul found himself in the vortex of intense family pressure as disgruntled family members expressed their annoyance at his decision, while pushing him to find another groom as soon as possible.

It was a difficult situation for him at home. Everyone except Karimul wanted the marriage to take place as the groom's family was more or less financially stable.

Liza, whose marriage proposal had inadvertently created so much tension at home, felt bad for the other members of her family, especially her mother, but deep down she was proud of her father for believing strongly in the rights of women and being against the dowry system. Despite being poor, her father had always been the epitome of honesty and humanity. Otherwise, he would not have struggled thus to work for others despite his own hardships.

Karimul knew he had made his own life difficult at home. If he could not find a good groom for his daughter, he would always be blamed for calling off Liza's wedding into a well-settled family. One day, when everyone was taking a siesta, Karimul gently patted Liza's forehand, asking her if she was very disappointed at her marriage being called off. Liza got up and hugged her father, who was weeping by then. She consoled him and told him how proud she was of him, that she would have rejected the groom anyway for demanding dowry as she did not want to get married into such a family.

Karimul was poor only financially, not morally or ethically. And all his children had grown up to be just like him. That day, Karimul felt immensely proud. His kids might not have received much of a formal education, but they did not lack in moral values, something he feels even today to be more important than degrees and certificates.

God helps those who tread the path of honesty and integrity. Eventually Karimul found a partner for Liza. Within a month of the marriage being called off, a relative once again initiated the process of finding a groom. They found a young man from a nearby village, Barobhuiya Bazaar, just a kilometre away from their home. The would-be groom's family members came to see her as the groom had declared he would marry the girl chosen by his parents and elders of his family. They met Liza and liked her. The boy was a cycle mechanic and they were very poor. But both Karimul and Liza liked the family and the would-be groom's attitude. Another thing was also clear: in spite of not being financially sound, the groom's side did not seek any dowry. Karimul agreed to the match at once.

The date for the marriage was fixed after Karimul visited the groom's house the next week. On returning from their house, Karimul started discussing the wedding preparations with his wife and Khalilur. With such a low income and no savings at all, how would Karimul get his daughter married? He was lost. But his elder brother, despite being angry with Karimul, told him not to worry and gave him the much-required confidence that everything would go smoothly. Karimul approached

Sukumar Das, the owner of the tea garden where Karimul works, who promised him some help. Help came from other sources too. He also borrowed money from some friends and relatives.

Finally, on a December night in 2003, Liza's wedding took place. It was a simple affair with the resources the family had managed to cobble together. Some villagers, close relatives and friends attended it.

When Liza was leaving with her husband, Karimul could not control his emotions and broke down, but he was happy that he had found a good life partner for his daughter. Liza might not have a financially well-off husband, but she would have a partner with good values. Besides, he had not given dowry for his daughter's marriage; he had not compromised on his principles.

After Liza's marriage, Karimul's main concern was to pay back the money he had taken for the wedding. For the next one and a half years, he worked overtime at the tea garden to repay the loan. He had no sooner done so than he found himself facing a similar challenge. His younger daughter, Shimu, now had to be married. They found a good match for her too—again someone who was not well-off. The young man, who was from Malbazar, worked as an assistant in a tailor shop. In September 2005, Shimu was married. Fortunately, this time Karimul did not face any problems related to dowry. But again, he had to seek help from the owner of the tea garden, Sukumar Das, as also from some friends, since his financial condition had remained unchanged.

Yet, despite his monetary woes, Karimul did not abandon his plan to buy a bike. Through all these trying times, the idea of buying a bike was at the back of his mind. He continued this struggle for almost eight years. Finally, around 2007, he made up his mind that come what may, he would buy a motorbike. In keeping with the adage, 'If there is a will, there is a way', Karimul found a way. He told different people about his idea of buying a motorbike and using it as an ambulance to ferry people to hospital. He spoke about it to Reyaj, as well as the owner of the tea garden. They agreed to lend him some money. He somehow managed Rs 14,000 from different people, which was the initial payment required. For the remaining amount (around Rs 60,000), he took a loan.

Karimul's dream had finally become a reality. When he placed his hands on the two-wheeler, his happiness knew no bounds. He broke down in joy and gratitude; he thanked God and his mother. He felt his mother had come back to him.

Thereafter, Karimul carried patients on his motorbike to Malbazar Sub-divisional Hospital, but if the patient was in a critical condition, he would ferry them to Jalpaiguri Sadar Hospital.

Jalpaiguri was at a distance of almost 45 kilometres from his home. Malbazar was closer, at 15 kilometres, but to reach the latter one had to cross the Chell. Crossing the river in the monsoons was an arduous task as the water level would rise. There was another approach to Malbazar, via Odlabari or Lataguri. But this route, too, was challenging after sunset: en route was a dense forest and, at night, wild animals would come out on the road. Karimul had often come face to face with elephants, bison and other animals while taking patients to a hospital at night.

Braving all this, Karimul took up the task of carrying patients to hospital on his bike as his mission in life. He felt that he was actually serving his mother when he ferried patients to the hospital. Therefore, whenever he got a call—be it night or day—to take a patient to the hospital, he would drop whatever he was doing and rush.

In its nascent stage, almost all great work or great thought attracts scepticism, or becomes the butt of jokes. When Karimul began using a motorbike as an ambulance, many people would crack jokes at his expense. From wondering how it could be called an ambulance to taunting him on his financial constraints to giving unsolicited advice about concentrating on his family, Karimul saw it all, heard it all, experienced it all. But he never heeded any of this: he was a man on a mission, and that mission was enough to motivate him to continue to serve the people of his area.

At that time, his salary at Subarnapur Tea Garden was Rs 3000. Almost one-third of his salary was spent in buying fuel for his motorbike. To this day, Karimul remains indebted to Reyaj and Sukumar Das for never deducting money from his salary for those days he was absent from work, taking the ailing and sick to hospital. Though he hardly goes to work these days, he still gets his salary from the tea garden, which he utilizes to serve people.

Till date, Karimul has ferried over 4000 patients to hospital on his bike. He has taken numerous attempted-suicide cases, as well as accident cases, to hospitals and helped them receive timely medical treatment. There have been cases where, despite his efforts, the patient couldn't be saved, when patients died on his bike on the way to hospital. He still remembers not being able to save the wife of his village friend Jahirul Islam. He was taking her to the hospital for childbirth when they had to stop and she gave birth to a baby in the middle of the road. But soon after delivery, she started bleeding profusely. Both mother and baby were taken to the hospital, but the mother died after a few hours. His friend Dilawar Hossain, who had suffered a brain stroke, also died en route to the hospital.

7

A Bike Ambulance Takes Shape

If I cannot do great things, I can do small things in a great way.

—Dr Martin Luther King, Jr[1]

Now that Karimul had a bike, he was no longer dependent on his cycle to ferry a patient. The bike gave the patients a greater chance of survival by ensuring they got to the hospital quickly. Karimul, too, was under less pressure, physically and mentally; he could be more certain of patients getting timely medical attention, be they sick or injured, and riding a motorbike was far less physically taxing than cycling all the way with a passenger.

[1] https://www.goodreads.com/quotes/313566-if-i-cannot-do-great-things-i-can-do-small.

One day, in 2008, when Karimul was enjoying a cup of tea with some acquaintances at a tea shop in Kranti Bazaar, one of them, Babu Mohanta, suddenly cried out. The engrossing discussion on political affairs was halted abruptly. The small group sprang into action to find out the reason behind Mohanta's shriek. Investigations revealed that a snake had bitten him just above the ankle. Karimul immediately made up his mind to identify the snake, as this would help the doctor decide on the course of treatment; it was imperative in such cases. He saw the snake but could not identify it. Thinking fast, he somehow caught the snake and put it in a small box so that he could carry it to the hospital. He applied a pressure bandage on the wound as well. With the help of those around them, Karimul got Mohanta tied to his back and asked a villager to ride pillion with him. Before starting out for Jalpaiguri Sadar Hospital, Karimul instructed the man to make sure that Mohanta did not fall sleep. The snake, carefully locked in the box, accompanied them to the hospital.

On the way, they met with a huge traffic jam on the bridge over the Teesta, just 5 kilometres from the hospital. The road was chock-a-block with vehicles stranded on the bridge, all trying to find a way out and, in the process, aggravating the situation. As Karimul zipped past the four-wheeled vehicles, he saw an ambulance stuck in the traffic.

When he asked the ambulance driver for the patient's details, he was told that the man had also been bitten by a snake, and they were heading for the same hospital as Karimul. Manoeuvring his much-smaller vehicle between the cars and moving towards the hospital with Mohanta, the soft-hearted Karimul felt sorry for the patient in the 'proper' ambulance, unable to get out.

Karimul soon reached the hospital. Once there, he showed the snake to the doctor, who was at first startled but then observed it intently for a few seconds before springing into action with the treatment.

After getting Mohanta admitted, Karimul went back to the bridge where they had seen the ambulance. He saw that the ambulance, along with other vehicles, was still there; the patient had, unfortunately, passed away.

After a couple of days, Babu Mohanta was released from the hospital. He was the first person bitten by a poisonous snake in the village to be saved—all because of Karimul's timely intervention and bike ambulance service.

Before this incident, though Karimul had ignored the taunts of some of the villagers and had gone about ferrying patients to hospital, he had sometimes harboured misgivings that his bike ambulance was a poor substitute for the conventional ambulance. But that day, he realized that his bike ambulance was sometimes far more convenient than a standard ambulance. From then on, there was no looking back for him. His new-found confidence enthused him to serve people with increased passion.

After he was awarded the Padma Shri, the Navayuvak Brindal Club, Siliguri, donated to him an ambulance that he used for some months. But the traditional ambulance not only consumed more fuel, it was also rather difficult to drive it to remote and far-flung areas. After some weeks, he stopped using that ambulance; though it is still with him, he doesn't use it. Instead, he now has three bike ambulances at home; one is used by his elder son, Raju, another by his younger son, Rajesh, while Karimul himself mostly uses the bike ambulance donated by Bajaj Auto, which has an attached carrier for patients.

Thanks to Karimul Hak's unique initiative, the bike ambulance has become popular in rural areas of India. Inspired by him, some social workers, as well as some NGOs, have started this service too, thereby saving thousands of lives in far-off areas of the country.

While Karimul has saved many lives, he deeply regrets not being able to save some. Still, he derives immense satisfaction from the fact that a person like him, with a paltry income and limited capacity, has made a difference in the lives of so many people. Relatives and family members of those who died en route to the hospital, or even after reaching the hospital, at least know that they, through Karimul, tried their best to save their loved one. This is a noteworthy achievement for Karimul, who dreams of a day when lack of medical treatment will not be the reason for someone's death.

8

A Coffin

It always seems impossible until it's done.

—Nelson Mandela[1]

Within a couple of years, most people in Kranti, Malbazar, Lataguri, Odlabari and different parts of Jalpaiguri district had come to know of the 24-hour, free bike ambulance service provided by Karimul Hak. By then, people had started calling him Bike Ambulance Dada. Whenever anyone needed an ambulance, they called him, and whatever time of the day or night it was, Karimul was there for them.

---

[1] https://www.usatoday.com/story/news/nation-now/2013/12/05/nelson-mandela-quotes/3775255/.

Whether he was having his lunch, or fast asleep at night, or dead tired after a day's hard work, Karimul would set aside his own needs and hasten to aid the suffering. Some days saw Karimul doing two consecutive trips to the hospital. True, he could have excused himself after a hectic day by saying he was exhausted or unwell, and perhaps no one would have objected, but Karimul never did that. For him, taking patients to the hospital, was—and still is—equal to serving his late mother, and this sentiment gave him the energy and strength to carry on the good work.

After he started his bike ambulance service, Karimul soon grew aware of many other problems in the healthcare sector in his village. Basic health facilities such as checking of blood pressure and blood sugar, provision of first aid to patients, and so forth were not available in the area. He began to pick up some basic medical knowledge from the doctors and then provide 'treatment' to poor people so they didn't have to go a long way to see a doctor for a minor issue. The doctors, most of whom he now shared a good rapport with, would give him medicines—free of cost—for simple ailments such as fever, cough, diarrhoea and minor stomach-related problems. At his behest, doctors also organized health awareness camps in his area. Occasionally, the health camps consisted of specialists from different medical backgrounds. The enterprising

Karimul would also set up 'health stalls' in fairs, football tournaments and different public places.

One day in March 2010, when Karimul was having his lunch, he got a call from the owner of Kranti Medical Hall at Kranti Bazaar. He urged Karimul to come as soon as possible, as the condition of a one-year-old infant had worsened and she had been referred to Jalpaiguri Sadar Hospital. He pushed away his plate and got ready to leave. His wife entreated him to finish his lunch and then go, but Karimul could not eat after hearing the news.

He hurried to Kranti Medical Hall where Santosh and Dipali Mondal, the girl's parents, were waiting anxiously. He asked them to accompany him on his bike, with their daughter. When they reached the hospital, the doctor declared the child brought dead. The parents were devastated. Karimul tried to console the traumatized young parents but in vain. Shattered, they cried bitterly at the realization that they would not see their daughter again. Karimul, reminded of his own daughter's death, also broke down. There is a special emotion that parents have for their first child: one becomes a father or a mother for the first time; it is a very tender feeling that is difficult to express. And if one's first child passes away, one can never forget or erase that agony.

Till date, Karimul remembers the day his daughter Lucky died due to lack of proper medical facilities in his area. When he had finally rushed his daughter to the hospital, it was too late.

Since this infant had died on her way to the hospital, the doctors wanted to carry out a post-mortem to ascertain the cause of death. While they took her body for the post-mortem, Karimul tried to arrange for an ambulance so that the parents could take the body back home. But the ambulance drivers demanded an amount that the unfortunate parents could not afford. After a lot of arguments, tears and pleadings, the girl's parents decided to leave their baby's body at the hospital and return with Karimul. Karimul did not approve of the idea, but he had no option. When they reached home, the girl's grandparents were livid with their son and daughter-in-law. They told them it was very important in Hindu rituals to perform the last rites.

This episode made Karimul ponder over a solution to this issue, should it happen again in the future—which was quite possible. He promised himself that nobody, in future, should have to face this kind of a heart-rending situation.

That is Karimul Hak for you. Whenever he sees a poor person grappling with any problem, he tries his utmost to solve it with whatever resources he has—he has never allowed his own lack of wealth to deter him. And invariably, at such times, when he desperately wanted to do something, someone or the other would come forward to support his cause. After some deep thinking, Karimul came up with a solution: a coffin. A coffin that could be attached to his motorbike, a coffin in which he would be able to carry the body if the relatives could not afford the conventional ambulance. He approached a few people he knew for some help. Some donated wood, some gave money. Soon, his plan of making a coffin became a reality. In 2011, he made a wooden box to which he attached two wheels of a cycle rickshaw.

Anyone could pull this coffin that Karimul had designed, or it could be attached to a motorbike. Whenever there was a need or a possibility that a body may have to be carried, the coffin came in handy. With this coffin, Karimul carried many bodies and helped countless local residents.

Nowadays, Karimul does not use this coffin, as Bajaj Auto presented him a specially designed bike ambulance in which he could carry patients, or the bodies of those who passed away.

9

Learning to Heal

Healthy citizens are the greatest asset any country can have.

—Winston Churchill[1]

After Karimul became a familiar sight in hospitals as the 'bike ambulance person', the doctors felt that if patients could be provided medical treatment earlier, chances of their recovery and survival would be greater. In some cases, it was also seen that patients who had been hastily brought to the hospital were actually not in a critical condition and did not need emergency attention. With this in mind, the doctors at the hospitals decided to give Karimul some basic healthcare tips, so that he could

---

[1] https://www.keepinspiring.me/winston-churchill-quotes/.

provide first-level medical care to patients before bringing them to the hospitals.

Dr Khiten Barman, who worked in Uttar Saripakuri Rural Health Centre at Kranti, near Karimul's house, had trained Karimul to check blood pressure and blood sugar, and how to use the stethoscope. Dr Soumen Mondal of Jalpaiguri Sadar Hospital taught him how to stitch up cuts in case someone met with an accident and needed immediate care. He also taught him how to dress injuries, cuts and boils. At the same time, Dr Mondal cautioned him that he should not stitch any sensitive body parts such as the eyes or eyebrows. Thereafter, Karimul was able to confidently treat patients—and there were many—who approached him with severe infections on their legs or hands.

Doctors at Jalpaiguri Sadar Hospital also explained to Karimul the symptoms of a heart attack, heart failure and brain stroke, and the dos and don'ts in such cases. They also carefully instructed him on the emergency procedure called CPR (cardiopulmonary resuscitation). Karimul also gave villagers vitamin B capsules, iron tablets and calcium supplements if he felt they needed it. But he was cautious, too: if he wasn't sure of the medicine or the dosage, he would call the doctors. In this way, he was able to provide relief to quite a few people.

The doctors also showed him how to use a nebulizer in case a patient suffering from breathing difficulties turned up at his doorstep. Since snakebites were a common occurrence in villages, they also taught him the correct way to handle such patients, what he should do, including that such patients must, if necessary, be forcefully kept awake en route to the hospital. This again made Karimul realize that his motorbike was an effective 'tool' for keeping such patients awake while he rushed them to the hospital. Over the years, Karimul has come across many such patients and saved them, too.

A dedicated student and quick learner, Karimul has also learnt how to detect malnutrition, how to treat it and advise patients, and the dos and don'ts that a pregnant woman should follow: from the food she should eat, to the rest she should get and the special attention that she needs. Karimul also always keeps an oxygen cylinder at home, and gives some to critically ill patients before ferrying them to the hospital. He has found this to be quite effective in easing the discomfort of patients, while giving them the necessary assurance that they would live to see another day.

Thanks to the doctors and NGOs who help him with free medicines, Karimul has a good supply. Occasionally, medical representatives give Karimul sample medicines. This way, Karimul has also operated his 'home clinic' in Dhalabari village for the past twelve years.

Karimul's promise to himself and his departed mother to provide medical care to the villagers did not end with his ambulance service. As we have seen, to provide holistic medical care and make villagers aware of health issues, Karimul has also conducted several health camps in many villages. He has organized camps on leprosy, AIDS and tuberculosis, which people saw—and, unfortunately, see even now—as infectious diseases. He has sensitized people about these diseases on several occasions, generating awareness and spreading knowledge of preventive measures and treatment procedures. His basic health service has helped almost one lakh people in his area.

Currently, Karimul is busy in the construction of a hospital adjacent to his house, which he hopes to develop as a model rural hospital where he can treat patients with the help of some eminent doctors.

10

Danger Ahead

Courage is the most important of all the virtues, because without courage you can't practice any other virtue consistently.

—Maya Angelou[1]

Karimul epitomizes the phrase 'when the going gets tough, the tough get going'. Karimul Hak's life has been one full of obstacles. Difficulties, hurdles and hardships have been his faithful companions in life—even to this date. Learned people and self-styled gurus tend to 'encouragingly' club all such as 'challenges', possibly because 'challenge' and

---

[1] *Maya Angelou: A Glorious Celebration* by Marcia Ann Gillespie, Rosa Johnson Butler, Richard A. Long.

'opportunity' are two sides of a coin. Had they met Karimul, they would have realized that here was one who was a living example of this concept. Despite the overwhelming problems that he has encountered, he has never buckled, never allowed his circumstances to get the better of him. Because he had—and still has—a mission in his life: the mission of taking the critically ill to hospitals and arranging treatment for them as early as possible. Whenever he has taken up any challenge in life, he has accomplished it.

The hospital closest to his village, Dhalabari, is the Malbazar Sub-divisional Hospital, a distance of 15 kilometres from his home. En route to Malbazar flows the Chell, which separates Kranti from the rest of the Malbazar block. Almost 2.5 lakh people reside in this area, where Karimul also lives.

During the non-rainy season, people go to Malbazar for various reasons, crossing the river which, like rivers in the hills, does not have much water in it. Karimul's motorbike also crosses the river almost every day with one patient or the other. But come monsoon, it is a different story altogether. The river swells because of the rains and crossing it becomes an uphill task, not to mention dangerous. There is another route to Malbazar, but it is a circuitous one, almost 45 kilometres from Kranti. This becomes a huge annoyance to the residents.

Of all the people, patients suffer the most. The critical patients, who are referred from rural hospitals to the district or town hospitals for better treatment, go through a harrowing time as they either have to go to Malbazar hospital or Jalpaiguri Sadar Hospital, which become equidistant due to the unavailability of a bridge over the Chell. Things become even more problematic at night, as not only does one have to negotiate one's way over the swollen river in the dark, but also a dense forest inhabited by wild animals.

Occasionally, Karimul has had to cross the river and go past the dense forest at night while taking critical patients to the hospitals. Due to the urgency of the situation, he was sometimes unable to take patients to Jalpaiguri. In such a scenario, Karimul had no option but to cross the Chell at night, especially in cases of attempted suicide or snakebite, where time plays an even greater role. While crossing the river, Karimul has, on numerous occasions, seen rhinos, leopards and herds of elephants or bison. The elephants are those he comes face to face with most regularly. But surprisingly, they have never attacked him.

Despite having acquired the status of a legend or a superman in and around his village, Karimul is, at the end of the day, a human being. On pitch-dark nights, on a road with a thick, silent forest all around, he would sometimes encounter these wild creatures only a few feet away from him. Karimul would get scared and fear for his life. Calming himself by praying to the Almighty for safety and protection was all that he could do, and did do. The animals would eventually go their way, and he, too, would continue down the road.

Maybe animals can also identify the goodness in him. Karimul has been a frequent traveller on these roads, biking past the dense jungle at night, risking his life to save those of others. When you work so selflessly for others, perhaps even nature helps you. Animals have never disturbed Karimul on his mission.

Not only wild animals, Karimul has had to face dreaded dacoits too. It was in 2011 that he was returning home at night after having admitted a patient at Jalpaiguri Sadar Hospital. It was a very dark, deserted stretch of road. All of a sudden, he was stopped by three armed men. But then one of the dacoits saw 'AMBULANCE' written on the front of the motorbike. He recognized Bike Ambulance Dada and alerted the others. Instead of robbing him or harming him in any way, they profusely begged his pardon for not having identified him earlier. Karimul just smiled and requested them not to involve themselves in crime and to serve humanity instead. Impressed, they gave him Rs 300, entreating him to utilize it for the poor.

This experience amazed Karimul. He again realized that despite initial scepticism, people respect and help someone who is working for the well-being of others. Another thing that he learnt that day was that everyone is inherently good. Maybe circumstances have led many of us to walk down the wrong path, but, given a chance, everyone can be convinced to work for the betterment of the society and the country. We just have to guide them down the right road and provide the necessary support. Or perhaps, many don't have a role model who can motivate them to do something good.

This is a huge crisis in our society right now: we don't have heroes to look up to. People like Karimul work silently. There are many Karimuls amongst us who are working tirelessly to make the world a better place to live in. Many people now know Karimul only because he was acknowledged by the Indian government, in the form of the Padma Shri. But there are numerous Karimuls whom we fail to honour in their lifetimes. It is high time that we honour our real heroes.

11

Branching Out

You have not lived today until you have done something for
someone who can never repay you.

—John Bunyan[1]

Karimul, who has been operating his free bike ambulance
service since 2007, had observed that there was a myriad of
healthcare issues of which he had no knowledge earlier. He
simply tackled the issues head-on using whatever seemed
the best option to him in the circumstances, and adapted
and adjusted to the pressures that his mission entailed.
Driven as he was by the goal of easing the suffering of poor

---

[1] *Living Well: Caring Enough to Do What's Right: A Guide to a Great*
   Life and World by Joseph M. Furner.

patients, he did not allow financial or other constraints to affect him. All he knew was that he had to carry on, to zealously pursue what he had set out to accomplish.

In fact, he had seen for himself that help did come one way or other; that's the beauty of doing something good for the society. If you really want to do something that benefits others, or maybe yourself, nobody can stop you from achieving it. You just need to have the determination and a never-say-die attitude. The rest is managed almost mystically.

One day, sometime in 2012, when Karimul was visiting a house in his village, he saw a differently abled boy, about twelve or thirteen years old, crying in a room. Karimul had gained enough expertise and experience by then to sense the reality of a situation; the child was unwanted, uncared for. Talking to the child's parents, he realized with a shock that they had lost all hope for their son's recovery and health, and were no longer concerned about his well-being. He was shaken. How could parents abandon their own children—this thought kept running through his mind. He walked into the boy's room and saw that the child, whose limbs had not developed properly, had been tied with a rope. Karimul untied him.

The boy reminded him of the time when he had broken his right leg in a bike accident. He had been confined to his room for six months, which had left him frustrated, stressed and agitated. Sometimes, he had wanted to break free. He could empathize with the boy, whose situation was so much worse—tied up and left in one room, day after day, perhaps even years.

That day he made another promise to his late mother, that he would do something for the differently abled people of his area. On asking around, he learnt that in his area alone there were at least fifteen such people. Over the next few days, Karimul visited the houses of the differently abled. All of them belonged to poor families and shared the same story: their families abused and neglected them. Living in such a toxic and hopeless environment, they had lost faith in others and looked upon themselves as liabilities.

Karimul took responsibility for all the fifteen such helpless people of his area. He spoke about their condition to the district administration, the district health department and some NGOs, and they all helped him in different ways. He managed tricycles for a few, while some others were given wheelchairs. Amongst those who were given a tricycle, two have since become financially self-sufficient, while one of them has set up a paan shop and another sells lottery tickets at Kranti Bazaar.

With some help, Karimul also built rooms for some of the differently abled people; now, they were not dependent on their families for anything, neither for food nor shelter.

He got differently abled children admitted to schools and purchased books for them. Hearing aids were provided to those who had difficulty in hearing. Karimul managed all these expenses with the help of government agencies, a few NGOs and some kind-hearted people.

To ensure their holistic well-being, Karimul would take out time every year from his busy schedule to take his 'adopted' family to participate in the annual sports meet of the physically challenged, which was organized by the Jalpaiguri Welfare Organization.

Once he had set in place his plans and programmes for the differently abled, Karimul turned his attention to old, destitute women. Some old women would occasionally approach him for medical treatment and share their stories of mistreatment by family members—they got neither food, nor clothes, nor respect. He saw his mother in all these impoverished women who suffered endlessly, and their tearful tales of disregard troubled him greatly. His mother's face, on that day when she was slowly but surely slipping away from them, would surface in his mind's eye, leaving him misty-eyed. Karimul often thought of taking steps that would ease the lives of these elderly women.

Gradually, Karimul shouldered responsibility for them as well. Now, as many as seventeen old ladies, who were abandoned by their families, are dependent on him. He handles everything: from providing them with food, clothes and even houses—with assistance from the local panchayat or Block Development Office—to complete free healthcare facilities.

Even so, he is not content with what he has achieved for the old women: he has set his sights on building a house for them, where they can live happily ever after.

12

Recognition

The happiest people I know are those who lose themselves in the service of others.

—Gordon B. Hinckley[1]

Karimul has seen poverty. Ever since his birth, poverty has been a constant factor in his life. But he is not alone. The entire area of Rajadanga, where the Haks have been living for years, has been under abject poverty.

For years, most people in Rajadanga have been daily wage labourers who worked in the farmlands. During the harvest season, they would find employment in the

---

[1] Greatest Motivational and Inspirational Quotes on Life, Love and Happiness.

fields, but at other times of the year they had to depend on odd jobs such as working in the houses of others, loading sand—collected from the banks of the Chell—in trucks, which Karimul, too, had done for many years. Since most of them failed to get work as wage labourers on a daily basis, they found it very hard to run their households.

With the establishment of tea gardens in that area, the employment situation improved—but only slightly. Some people like Karimul got full-time employment in the tea gardens, but the overall scenario in and around Karimul's village still remains grim. Even now, most of the houses are dilapidated. The roofs of most houses are in such bad shape that in the rainy season it's very difficult to save oneself from getting drenched. During winter, the indoors offer barely any respite from the severity of the cold. Many people have neither sweaters nor blankets to keep themselves warm. Nor do they have enough food to keep their bellies full and their spirits high. While adults can be seen in well-worn and patched-up clothes, the children remain mostly unclad.

Though Karimul's situation was no better than that of the others, sensitive as he was, the plight of others tormented him. He had cherished a deep desire to make a difference in the lives of these people. When he started his mission of ferrying people to hospitals, he knew he was working on just one issue; the other numerous problems in his region were constantly at the back of his mind, and he was well aware that these too demanded a solution. The Padma Shri opened the door for him to work in other spheres of peoples' lives. Now, many people, social organizations and NGOs routinely come to his house and donate blankets and winter clothes.

Though the Padma Shri took Karimul himself by surprise, there had been a build-up to the award. Karimul's efforts first received appreciation in 2012, when he was conferred with the Ananya Samman by Zee News in Kolkata. Before that, he was known only to the people of Jalpaiguri district for his social work for critically ill patients. It was only after the Ananya Samman that he attracted the attention of people in West Bengal and some other parts of the country. Before the award, a team from Zee had come to his house to shoot a documentary on him. That was another first for Karimul—being in front of a camera. He admitted this had been a rather unnerving experience for him.

The Ananya Samman motivated Karimul to put in even more effort and hours for the poor and downtrodden. He worked with renewed vigour. He ferried more patients to different hospitals; organized health camps more frequently; and so forth. News of his noble service would be regularly featured on different local news channels and in various newspapers of West Bengal. Karimul's mission had caught the attention of the media.

After the Ananya Samman, Karimul's next big moment of recognition came in 2014, when he was called to participate in *Dadagiri*, a popular Bengali quiz show on Zee Bangla. It was anchored by former captain of the Indian cricket team, the charismatic Sourav Ganguly. Karimul's popularity rose to new heights. Ganguly, a legend both in West Bengal and the country, warmly appreciated Karimul's work on the show and wrote a special message for him in the certificate that Karimul received during the programme: 'May God give you strength so that you can work more for the people.'

Karimul believes that Ganguly's prayer acted as a charm for him, because thereafter, his life started to change gradually with accolades pouring in for his selfless work.

Even as he focused on his life's quest, some very important events unfolded in Karimul's family life. From 2003 to 2014, till he finally got recognition on a bigger platform, Karimul had to sort out major challenges on the family front. Apart from arranging the marriages of his two daughters, Karimul also had the responsibility of settling his two sons. Though they could not study much due to the family's financial hardships, they were, by and large, smart boys. In 2008, Raju rented a small shop in Kranti Bazaar to sell make-up items and essential goods. Karimul's younger son Rajesh, who, too, had not been able to clear Class X, did a course on mobile repairing in Jalpaiguri and opened a mobile repairing shop in Kranti Bazaar. When both his sons started earning, Karimul decided to get them married. Raju got married in 2012 and Rajesh in 2014.

On the one hand, Karimul was serving the poor by taking critically ill patients to hospital and, on the other, he had to take care of several responsibilities in the family. Through it all, as Karimul juggled and balanced his job at the tea garden, his service to the poor and the duties of a father, he believes the powerful Almighty stood by him, quietly providing the required support.

13

Double Whammy

Those who don't know how to suffer are the worst off. There are times when the only correct thing we can do is to bear out troubles until a better day.

—Deng Mìng-Dao[1]

Thanks to the reports published in different media, people had begun to recognize Karimul Hak and his bike ambulance. He had received the Ananya Samman in 2012 and also participated in the TV show *Dadagiri* in 2014. Yet, though he continued to help people through his bike ambulance service, there was no appreciable change in his

---

[1] https://quotes.pub/q/those-who-dont-know-how-to-suffer-are-the-worst-off-there-ar-457828.

financial status. His sons, who were married by then, were running small shops in Kranti Bazaar. With a salary of Rs 4000 by this time, Karimul continued to live a poor man's life with his family members who, though, hardly complained.

Pain, tragedy and suffering have never deserted Karimul in his eventful life journey. Every few years, he has faced one trauma or the other—hunger throughout his childhood; not earning enough as a daily wage labourer in his early adult life to cover even the bare necessities; death of his firstborn because of wrong treatment; a motorbike accident which left him with a slight limp; his mother's death because of lack of medical treatment. And then another blow fell.

In 2014, his first grandchild, nine-month-old Farhan, the son of his elder son Raju, was diagnosed with leukaemia. Farhan had had fever for some time; it would go away after basic medication, only to return after a few days. When this continued for about twenty days, Raju took Farhan to Jalpaiguri Sadar Hospital and consulted a doctor, who advised some blood tests. Raju left his wife, Chhabina Begum, and Farhan at his wife's maternal house at Denguajhar Tea Estate—close to Jalpaiguri town where Farhan was undergoing treatment—and returned to his Dhalabari home.

On that fateful day, when the family heard the devastating news, Karimul was out distributing clothes in a closed tea garden. Since he was in a remote area and inside a tea garden, the hospital staff could not contact him. Around 10 p.m., the hospital was finally able to get in touch with Karimul. Farhan's blood reports indicated a life-threatening disease; he needed to be hospitalized immediately. Karimul reached home and broke the news to his family. Accompanied by his wife, Anjuwara, and Raju, they went directly to Denguajhar Tea Estate, from where they picked up little Farhan and Chhabina, and headed to the hospital.

The doctor at the hospital told them that Farhan's blood cancer needed urgent attention. They referred him to North Bengal Medical College and Hospital in Siliguri, about 50 kilometres away. When they finally reached the hospital, it was around 2 a.m. Aware of Karimul's financial plight, an acquaintance had given him some money before they had set out for Jalpaiguri, which enabled him to hire an ambulance for Farhan.

Farhan was admitted right away in North Bengal Medical College. His platelet count was very low and he had to be given some urgently. Karimul had only asked a few of his friends and Raju's friends to donate platelets, but a great number of people turned up.

Throughout his life, Karimul had never cared much about his own and his family's well-being. Despite his own troubles, he had put others in need first. This time, the man who had got so many people out of trouble was himself in trouble. Most of the time in our lives we get what we give. When we give love, we get love. When we spread hatred and anger, we get those same things in return. It is often observed that when you do something good for people without any expectations, you get the same in return. People came in huge numbers and helped Karimul out during one of his toughest personal battles.

The next morning, he approached the president of the Jalpaiguri Welfare Association for financial help. The local media also supported him during this time with extensive media coverage of his grandson's disease and his appeal for financial help. Different social organizations raised money for Karimul during this time. He is especially thankful to Mampi Adhikari, a social worker based in Maynaguri, who helped him raise Rs 11,000. He still remembers a gesture by a rickshaw puller who donated Rs 100 during the fund-raising programme in Maynaguri. Another social organization held a fund-raising programme in Jalpaiguri and collected Rs 50,000 for him. A pathological laboratory in Siliguri did all the tests for Farhan, free of cost.

As Farhan's treatment started, and he responded to it, getting better at North Bengal Medical College, the Hak family faced yet another crisis. And this time it was the indefatigable Karimul himself who was affected. After staying with Farhan at the hospital for a week, Karimul returned to his village after getting a call from a patient back home, leaving Raju and Chhabina with Farhan. Karimul took the patient to Jalpaiguri Sadar Hospital during the day and came back home in the evening.

He was feeling very tired that day and decided to take a nap; his wife was busy preparing dinner. By the time Anjuwara had finished cooking, it was 9 p.m. She went to call Karimul for dinner but saw him lying on the bed, with something oozing from his mouth. Anjuwara immediately raised an alarm, and Rajesh, who was in the next room, rushed in to see what had happened. They realized that this time it was Karimul who would have to be taken to the hospital.

They did not waste time, and Anjuwara also accompanied Rajesh to Jalpaiguri Sadar Hospital. After examining Karimul, the doctor admitted Karimul to the ICU. He had suffered a heart attack.

When Raju got the news, he desperately wanted to go to Jalpaiguri, to be by his father's side. Since his son was recovering well and feeling a lot better, Raju hastened to see his father, leaving his wife by Farhan's side. Raju found his father in a critical condition. The doctor treating his father told Raju that Karimul's condition would have been worse if there had been any delay in bringing him to the hospital. The next ten days were tough for Raju: both his father and son had been hospitalized—in two different hospitals in two different towns.

After seven days, Karimul was shifted to the general ward as his condition stabilized. When he was discharged from the hospital after fifteen days, the doctor asked Karimul to consult a prominent cardiologist for better treatment. But Karimul did not follow this advice as he was sure he had recovered. He did not give it a second thought, despite knowing several specialists, including the legendary Dr Devi Shetty. Nowadays, even though Karimul meets cardiologists, calls them, sends poor patients to them, he somehow always forgets his own problem. His family's and well-wishers' pleas to consult a cardiologist simply fall on deaf ears; his friends fear that it may prove to be fatal in the future.

After his discharge from hospital, Karimul had gone to see Farhan in Siliguri, where doctors advised him to go back home and take proper rest. When Farhan was discharged, his doctor advised medication for at least a few years. Farhan needed blood transfusion at regular intervals and his chances of complete recovery were very high since the disease had been detected early.

Karimul, taking the advice of his well-wishers, took an appointment for Farhan's treatment with a doctor in Kolkata's NRS Medical College and Hospital. The doctor drilled into them that Farhan had to strictly follow the medication for the next few years. Karimul, who had not been able to save Lucky all those years ago, did save Farhan with timely medical intervention.

Four years have since passed. Farhan is almost fine now and has grown up to be a delightful child who keeps his family members on their toes with his antics.

14

A Secular Indian

The sovereignty of scriptures of all religions must come to an end if we want to have a united integrated modern India.

—B.R. Ambedkar[1]

Karimul has based his life on Swami Vivekananda's words, '*Jibe prem kore jei jon, sei jon sebiche Ishwar*' (If you want to serve God, serve humanity). He considers the life, works and words of this great Indian monk to be his biggest motivation. Karimul's life philosophy has been to serve humanity, not any religion, caste or creed. Believing firmly that when people suffer, humanity suffers, his aim in life has been to relieve his fellow beings of pain and misery.

---

[1] http://drishti-magazine.org/2018/sparkle/articles/article.php?id=2.

When he gets a call to ferry a sick or injured person to hospital, Karimul's immediate response is to serve the one in need; unlike many in today's world, his decision is not based on the religion or caste of that person. For him, everyone is a part of the one God who does not belong to any particular religion.

One incident in 2015 highlights Karimul's secular character. He had set up a health check-up stall in Bhandari Mela near his home. During these fairs, a group of people stay together and sing religious songs sitting adjacent to a temple, around which the local fair is held. Most of them are generally Vaishnavas, with some Brahmins joining in, too. The devotees give them food, money and other essentials, and the group stays there for the entire duration of the fair. This kind of fair runs for three or four days, sometimes for a week, and sometimes even for a month.

On the very first day of the fair, while conducting health check-ups of the villagers, Karimul came across an old woman, lying alone, crying. He learnt that she had been abandoned by the Vaishnavas she had come to the fair with. Further inquiry revealed that the old woman was suffering from diarrhoea and had dirtied the place. For this reason, she had been thrown out by her group. Ever compassionate, Karimul took her to his medical stall, gave her some medicines and asked her to sit there till she felt well. Karimul took the onus on himself to clean the area she had dirtied.

He then went home for lunch, but while eating he got the news that a woman of his village had set herself on fire. Karimul hurried to take the woman to Jalpaiguri Sadar Hospital. When he returned to the fair in the evening, he was pleased to find that the old woman was slightly better. But he discovered that she hadn't eaten anything the entire day. Disturbed, Karimul went home, got Anjuwara to prepare some rice, returned to the fair with it and fed the old woman. That was one of the most satisfying days for him as serving the old, abandoned lady gave him the same satisfaction as serving his mother.

Next morning, when he reached the fair, he was delighted to see the old woman fully fit. She hugged him and started to cry. Karimul, too, grew emotional. Even now, the old woman comes to the fair every year; Karimul checks her health and gives her clothes.

Karimul was saddened by the attitude of the group of Vaishnavas who had abandoned the old woman, a member of their group. On the face of it, they served God, but they could not serve an old, helpless woman who needed assistance. When he met the Vaishnavas, he told them that God cannot be reached by merely singing songs; to realize God, all they have to do is serve mankind.

For Karimul, helping the downtrodden was—and still is—equivalent to serving the country. According to him, a doctor, an engineer or a government officer do not belong to any religion. Rather, they serve every human being—Hindus, Muslims, Christians, Sikhs, Buddhists and followers of all the other religions—of the country. He regrets that we don't follow our own Constitution, which talks about secularism. He strongly rues Mohammad Ali Jinnah's push for a separate nation in the name of religion and is convinced that this is the source of all the problems in the region, something for which we are still paying the price.

Fake appeasement in the name of religion, or creating unrest by stirring religious sentiments, as some narrow-minded politicians do for their own vested interests, angers Karimul immensely as it derails the progress of the nation. Likewise, the misinterpretation of Islam by several preachers upsets him, as they are simply sowing seeds of disharmony and discontent in society, and weakening the country. Karimul holds the view that a good Muslim can't be involved in violence, that Islam does not support this. He also believes that helping people out of their pain and agony makes one more pious than following the customs of a devout Muslim. He has never gone to Haj, but he serves Allah by serving the poor and hapless.

Karimul, whose life has been an example of secularism, has never felt that he is just a Muslim. He is regularly invited as a chief guest to inaugurate different religious programmes, such as Durga Puja, Ganesh Puja and others. Once, he was called upon to inaugurate a Hindu temple. He has not only entered temples, but has performed puja, too. Karimul can even recite shlokas from the Gita and Upanishads.

In fact, one of Karimul's dearest friends is Aditya Debsharma, a Hindu priest who lives in Kranti, and whose mother loves Karimul dearly. Indeed, the entire family encourages and admires Karimul for his selfless work for the people of the area. A frequent visitor to their house, he is often invited for meals by the family.

As said earlier, the Haks have always been broad-minded and progressive. Upholding the central government's stand against the triple talaq system, Karimul also feels strongly about the education of Muslim girls; he believes it will bring about a paradigm shift in their social status and improve Indian society, too.

Karimul Hak at the ceremony to receive the Padma Shri at Rashtrapati Bhavan, New Delhi.

Karimul receiving the honour from former President Pranab Mukherjee.

Karimul with his taekwondo team members.

With the people he helps regularly.

Karimul distributing clothes to the poor.

During a medical camp at Karimul's house.

Karimul in front of the upcoming hospital next to his house.

Karimul with all his awards of recognition.

Tokens of appreciation.

15

In the Limelight

When you want something, all the universe conspires in helping you to achieve it.

—Paulo Coelho[1]

Karimul has been ferrying the sick since 1999, first on his bicycle and then on his bike ambulance from 2007. It was something he loved doing—he was simply following his heart. He had never thought of becoming popular, or receiving any awards for his work. But when newspapers and news channels started covering Karimul's

---

[1] https://en.wikiquote.org/wiki/Paulo_Coelho#The_Alchemist_ (1988).

life and work, people gradually got to know about this extraordinary, yet simple man.

But his story did not cross the borders of West Bengal before 2016, until Bajaj V, the motorbike that was built using a partial amount of scrap metal from the decommissioned INS Vikrant, launched an initiative called 'Invincible Indians: Stories That Invoke Pride Everyday'.[2] This was a unique effort to unearth stories of ordinary Indians who, by their sheer grit, fortitude and guts performed extraordinary acts to serve society.

To bring the selfless service of such people into the limelight, Bajaj Auto released five digital documentaries, conceptualized and created by Leo Burnett India. The films portrayed the lives of five 'invincible Indians': Vijaylakshmi Sharma, Om Prakash Sharma, Chewang Norphel, Bipin Ganatra and Karimul Hak.

Vijaylakshmi Sharma, who hails from Bhojpur village of Phagi district of Rajasthan, fights against child marriage. She campaigns from door to door in her village and the surrounding areas to stop child marriages, despite being dogged by threats. Om Prakash Sharma, popularly called 'Medicine Baba', collects unused medicines from houses in the National Capital Region (NCR) and gives them to those who can't afford basic healthcare. 'The Iceman' is

---

[2] https://www.youtube.com/watch?v=HPMi42iAJeA.

the story of Chewang Norphel of Ladakh. He took up the challenge of solving Ladakh's water crisis by creating fifteen artificial glaciers. In 2015, he was awarded the Padma Shri. Bipin Ganatra, popularly called 'Aagun Pakhi' (Firebird), has devoted his life to saving people from fires. Having undergone the trauma of seeing his brother burn to death, Ganatra works as a volunteer firefighter with the Kolkata Fire Department.

The story of Karimul Hak fit the bill perfectly, as his work was related to the motorbike. Bajaj found Karimul Hak, the man who took patients to hospital on his motorbike, to be the most apt for the promotion of the Bajaj V motorbike. The team came to his village and stayed at a nearby resort for seven days to shoot the documentary. After that, Karimul was taken to Nashik, where he was given a bike ambulance specially designed for him. The last scene of the documentary, where he is seen removing the cloth covering the bike, was a genuine one, not staged. The team had not disclosed to Karimul that he would be given this new bike ambulance. He was taken to a room where a large object lay hidden under a cloth. He was then asked to remove the cloth. Karimul did as he was told, and when he saw the specially designed bike ambulance that could comfortably carry a patient, he broke down. The scene is captured wonderfully in the documentary, and Karimul's reaction is likely to tug at the heartstrings of anyone watching it. Fitted with a waterproof stretcher and ports for oxygen cylinders, the specially designed Bajaj V15 motorcycle ambulance is now his faithful companion.

Bajaj launched their 'Invincible Indians' campaign in the middle of 2016. Everything happened very quickly thereafter. Karimul's story transcended the borders of West Bengal and reached all corners of the nation. All of a sudden, the focus of the national media was on him. National TV channels like India Today and NDTV did stories on him. Even an international news channel like Al Jazeera ran a story on 'Bike Ambulance Dada'.[3]

The little-known hero's story soon went viral, penetrating as far as the office of the President of India. He was flooded with calls from Delhi, Mumbai and even outside the country. People started calling him on the phone and offering help. Sometimes, the callers spoke in English, a language he didn't know.

With word of Karimul's mission reaching the higher echelons of the Indian government, his name was announced for the Padma Shri. Most people who know him closely, as well as Karimul himself, admitted that the Bajaj 'Invincible Indians' story changed his life too quickly. That happens in life. It may take time, but when you work

---

[3] https://www.youtube.com/watch?v=HjdxFtaZIBU.

selflessly for the others, you are definitely rewarded for your good deeds.

Whatever the circumstances and whoever recommended his name, one thing is certain: The Government of India has done a commendable job in conferring the Padma Shri upon a man who has worked tirelessly for twenty years to serve the poor.

16

Two Units of Blood, Please!

When you forgive, you in no way change the past—but you sure do change the future.

—Bernard Meltzer[1]

Karimul was basking in his new-found glory after the Padma Shri, going about his work for poor villagers with renewed vigour and zeal. Everything was going well, but then disaster struck, again.

On 26 October 2017, Karimul was on the way to Malbazar Hospital with a pregnant lady. He was feeling somewhat tired that day, perhaps because he had organized a blood donation camp the previous day in Kranti. Since

---

[1] https://www.brainyquote.com/quotes/bernard_meltzer_132866.

blood donation camps involved a lot of careful overseeing, organizing, they drained him. Blood donors had turned up in large numbers and almost 100 units of blood had been donated.

En route to the hospital, Karimul got a call from Anjuwara. Their younger daughter, Shimu Begum, who was staying with them at that time because of her pregnancy, had slipped and fallen in the bathroom. Shimu, who was five months pregnant, was bleeding profusely. His wife asked him to return immediately as she did not know what to do. Shimu's husband and Karimul's sons were also not around. Karimul was needed at home to help his daughter. He was in a dilemma. On the one hand, his daughter was in a critical condition. On the other hand, he was carrying a patient to the hospital. How could he leave her?

After some thought, Karimul decided that his duty towards the patient took priority over everything else. He called Raju, explained the situation, and asked him to take care of Shimu until his return. Raju hastened home and took Shimu to Jalpaiguri Sadar Hospital, where she was admitted to the ICU as her condition had deteriorated after the heavy bleeding. After an hour or so, a visibly tense Karimul reached the hospital. The doctor explained to him the gravity of the situation and asked him to arrange for O+ve blood as soon as possible. He also warned that failure to do so would mean endangering Shimu's life.

First, they arranged one unit of blood from the blood bank. Later, the doctor asked him to come with one more unit. Karimul, who was also carrying his donor's card, asked for one more unit of blood from the blood bank staff. But the person in charge flatly refused to give him more blood, instead asking him to bring a donor—and even then, he was informed, there was no guarantee about blood being available. Taken aback, the desperate Karimul again pleaded for the blood, explaining his daughter's grave condition. He even mentioned the blood donation camp he had organized just the previous day, but his plea fell on deaf ears. In fact, the person in question responded rudely and jeered at him. He was shocked; the board outside the blood bank declared that four units of O+ve blood were in stock, yet the staff refused to give him one unit, claiming there was no blood.

Some mediapersons got wind of Karimul's situation and sped to the hospital to cover the news. And suddenly, all hell broke loose! That someone who had selflessly done so much for people, who had organized so many blood donation camps, and who had worked tirelessly to provide basic healthcare facilities to the poor had been so shamefully treated for asking for a unit of blood for his own daughter, angered the public.

The local MP, Bijoy Chandra Barman, hurried to visit Karimul's daughter at the hospital and assured him that strict action would be taken in this regard. He asked the hospital authority to conduct an inquiry. Soon, the West Bengal Health Department jumped on the bandwagon, demanding that necessary action be taken. Next, the then district magistrate of Jalpaiguri, Rachna Bhagat, stepped in, asking the hospital administration to look into the matter.

Well-wishers from social organizations came forward and volunteered to donate blood for Shimu. Karimul was touched by their generosity and support. However, despite persistent urgings to officially complain against the staff member, he refused. Instead, through the media, he requested all blood bank staff to generally behave politely with the common people and cooperate with them.

While the incident again demonstrated the depth of Karimul's popularity in this region, it also served as an eye-opener. If a person like Karimul Hak, a Padma Shri awardee, found it so difficult to get blood in time for his critically ill daughter, then one can well imagine what the common people of India—especially the poor and marginalized, who need more assistance than most others—have to go through every day to avail of services they are entitled to and which have been put in place for them. It exposed the huge gaps in the country's basic healthcare facilities for the poor, which need to be tackled urgently. Lakhs of people die every year in India because they don't get timely medical service.

Shimu was discharged after ten days; however, in spite of their best efforts, the doctors could not save the baby.

17

A Selfie with the Prime Minister

It is very difficult for the prosperous to be humble.

—Jane Austen[1]

In November 2017, eight months after Karimul was awarded the Padma Shri, he received a letter from Rashtrapati Bhavan, inviting him for the year's 'At Home' reception on 26 January 2018, on the occasion of Republic Day. Every year, on Independence Day and Republic Day, the President holds an 'At Home' ceremony at Rashtrapati Bhavan, to which the prime minister and his cabinet, the leader of the Opposition, MPs and all the Padma awardees of that year are invited.

---

[1] https://www.brainyquote.com/quotes/bernard_meltzer_132866.

It is a dream invitation for anyone, but Karimul did not have enough money to go to Delhi. After discussing the matter with his family, he decided to skip it. However, the news of his inability to be present at the prestigious event was published in different newspapers and, subsequently, different news channels, too, covered it.

As soon as this news got out, help poured in from several quarters. Two social organizations came forward to help him. They bought round-trip flight tickets for him and convinced Karimul to attend the event, as they saw it as a not-to-be-missed opportunity to meet both the President and prime minister of the country. Before leaving for Delhi, Karimul addressed the media in Siliguri. He promised that, if possible, he would inform the prime minister about the lack of basic healthcare facilities in the region, and request him for a hospital on the lines of Delhi's AIIMS (All India Institute of Medical Sciences) in north Bengal. Perforce, residents here had to travel to other parts of the country for treatment, which significantly increased their financial burden and stress. He said he would also urge for the construction of a bridge over the Chell.

Karimul checked into a hotel in New Delhi the day before the programme. On the day of the event, since he did not have the luxury of taking a cab, he boarded a bus, which took him close to Raisina Hill. From there, he walked to Rashtrapati Bhavan. However, he was stopped at the main gate. On being questioned, Karimul informed the security personnel that he was an invitee to the 'At Home' event, but they were not convinced. Their suspicion was natural: who on earth *walked* to such a prestigious, high-profile event!

Ironically, Karimul was carrying the free parking slip that had been sent along with the invitation card. He showed the invite, as well as the parking slip, to the guards. They then contacted the authority concerned inside Rashtrapati Bhavan, who confirmed Karimul's invitation. Finally, he was permitted to enter the hallowed grounds of Rashtrapati Bhavan.

That year, the 'At Home' reception was truly a special event, as ten chief guests—the heads of the ASEAN (Association of Southeast Asian Nations) countries—all the union ministers, former prime minister Manmohan Singh, former vice president Hamid Ansari and former Congress president Rahul Gandhi were present, along with the heads of the Indian defence forces and the Padma Shri awardees.

Not only did Karimul feel shy at such an august occasion, but he was also lost as he had no experience whatsoever of attending events of this magnitude, glamour and significance. To add to his misery, he did not know English. Suddenly, he saw Prime Minister Modi on his way down the barricaded receiving line. The prime minister spotted Karimul and stopped to chat with him. Karimul was awestruck and did not know what to do. He finally asked the prime minister for a selfie. Modi readily agreed, but as Karimul fumbled with his phone—he was not very comfortable with a smartphone—the prime minister took the phone from him and took the selfie. Later, Karimul also took selfies with Rahul Gandhi and two of the defence chiefs.

Talking to the media later, Karimul had said, 'I wanted a picture with the prime minister, but I am not very handy with the phone. Prime Minister Modi then took the picture from my phone. After that, without any prompting, he inquired about my bike ambulance service. He also asked me whether the bridge that I had wanted to be built—to cross our village to several other interior areas—had been constructed. I had told him last year that the bridge would ease our commute. I told him we were still waiting for it and he promised it would be done soon.' Expressing his delight, Karimul had added, 'I am happy that he remembered and I feel that we will get our bridge soon.'

For Karimul, it was a dream come true. Till date, he can't believe that the prime minister remembered an ordinary person like him. What struck him most was that the prime minister had asked him about the bridge over the Chell. He is certain that there is 'something extra' about Prime Minister Modi which sets him apart from all other leaders. So fascinated is he with this meeting with the prime minister that wherever he goes, he happily shares his 'selfie story'.[2]

---

[2] https://www.thehindu.com/news/national/may-i-do-the-honours-asks-modi-for-selfie-with-a-padma-shree/article22530066.ece.

18

Beti Padhao, Beti Bachao

If you educate a man, you educate an individual; but if you educate a woman, you educate an entire family.

—Mahatma Gandhi[1]

Karimul did not realize the value of education as a child. He now regrets not taking his studies seriously. But deeper than this runs the regret that none of his children completed their formal education, only because of financial constraints.

Later in life, when Karimul was working in the healthcare sector, his lack of education affected him deeply. That he found it difficult to read the name of medicines

---

[1] https://www.mkgandhi.org/articles/mahatma-and-women.html.

or understand the composition of a particular medicine disheartened him. Now, he can read, but just about.

This is the reason why—apart from primary healthcare, in which he works—Karimul wants to transform the education scenario in rural areas. Rural folk are still not particular about education. Young people who come from financially weak families, or whose parents are illiterate, are often made to do different jobs, mostly in the unorganized sector, early in life so that they can contribute to the family kitty. Naturally, the drop-out rate is still alarmingly high in such cases.

In his own village, Karimul had seen several children dropping out of school and noted that their parents did nothing to prevent them from doing so. Children who had cleared the Class XII board exams often opted out of further studies because of financial reasons. Girls were, and still are, especially neglected as most parents consider daughters as liabilities to be married off as soon as they turn fifteen or sixteen. A visionary man, Karimul views girls as the backbone of the family, as well as of the society. If girls are not well educated, the family will not be able to sustain itself, neither will it ever be able to uplift itself, he believes.

Sometimes, the girls in his village or adjoining villages come to him and request him to help them continue their studies. Seeing their commitment, he decided to do something for them.

In early 2017, he had got a call from Pune. The caller was Subhamoy Ghosh, an IT consultant. Originally from West Bengal, Subhamoy had shifted to Pune for professional reasons. When he was younger, Subhamoy had seen how talented students failed to do well in life due to lack of support and opportunity. After setting up his own establishment, Subhamoy had started helping poor students in different parts of West Bengal. For some time, he had been looking for a dedicated and honest person in Jalpaiguri district, who worked at the grassroots level. After reading about Karimul, he contacted him. Subhamoy requested Karimul to provide him with the names of some students whom he could help.

Karimul, in turn, told him about a few girls who were finding it difficult to continue their studies because of financial constraints. He requested Subhamoy to help them.

Initially, Subhamoy took full financial responsibility of Madhabi Roy, who is currently on the verge of completing her civil engineering degree. Since then, Subhamoy has taken up the academic responsibility for more girls. He has visited Karimul's house and the houses of all the girls whose education he is sponsoring. Now, he donates money for ten girls who are pursuing various degree courses. He also supports the education of two visually challenged students, a boy and a girl. Inspired by Karimul's mission in life,

Subhamoy has been sending around Rs 20,000 a month for the education of these poor students, who otherwise would have quit studying by now.

Another educational initiative in which Karimul has played a role is the Vidya Charcha Kendra, a one-teacher, tutorial-type school where an educated woman (who has cleared at least Class X) of the village teaches small children. She earns around Rs 1000 per month as salary and imparts basic education to very poor children in the age group of three to seven years. A brainchild of Sutanu Bhattacharya, a former professor of economics at Kalyani University of West Bengal, it is an attempt to bring economically backward children into mainstream education, though it has nothing to do with typical education.

Professor Bhattacharya felt that the current school syllabus did not take care of the needs of underprivileged children. Hence, he developed a specially designed syllabus and a unique style of teaching/learning to help these children. A child may or may not go to school, but in the Vidya Charcha Kendra they are taught the rudiments of mathematics, English and Bengali. The books are specifically designed for the tutors, so that they can make learning easy for little children. Apart from helping village kids, this initiative has one more purpose. It is empowering village women as well. Generally, the kendras are run with the help of different donors.

Towards the end of 2017, Dhiman Das, a student of Professor Bhattacharya, contacted Karimul and expressed his organization's desire to open such schools. Karimul, who by then had started working in the education sector, readily accepted the proposal and asked Das to visit his village and the neighbouring ones with other members of his organization. After their visit, the members decided to open six centres in January 2018. Recently, they added two more centres, making it a total of eight.

Karimul, who works as a mentor in these schools, is pleased that poor children are benefiting through the Vidya Charcha Kendras. He wants more people to come forward and help in running the schools so that they can start more of these, and in as many villages as possible.

Apart from these efforts, Karimul has also started imparting vocational training to the women in his village with the help of his two daughters. After a benefactor donated seven sewing machines, his elder daughter, Liza, took sewing courses for seventeen women of their village, so that they could become self-sufficient. Karimul hopes to organize such vocational training on a larger scale in the future. Additionally, he plans to gather a group of women and get them trained in making wooden furniture, to be sold in different markets. For this, he has envisioned constructing a building in the village, which will function as the centre for imparting vocational training courses for women.

Like all visionary people, he has a modern take on education, as well as women's empowerment. He strongly believes that if we don't encourage women to become educated or self-sufficient, our country will never prosper as a fully developed nation.

Besides education and training for women, Karimul considers self-protection to be an equally important aspect for them. Being physically strong is imperative for everyone. He specifically wants all girls to learn self-defence so that they can confidently step out of their homes, for work or fun. When crimes against women have become a daily phenomenon in the country, he wants women to make their own security arrangements. That's why he has also started a taekwondo training centre at his home. Two taekwondo teachers come from Jalpaiguri and train almost fifty poor children of his area. Recently, Lions Club of Siliguri Dignity donated taekwondo uniforms to these children.

Karimul's efforts towards education, especially girls' education, and self-defence have earned him plenty of praise.

19

Troubles Brew in Tea Gardens

No one is useless in this world who lightens the burdens of another.

—Charles Dickens[1]

The northern part of Bengal, where Karimul lives, has been known mainly for its three Ts—tea, timber and tourism. India has, over time, become the second largest tea producer in the world; the northeast region, including the northern part of West Bengal, is among the world's top tea producers.

---

[1] https://www.goodreads.com/quotes/18876-no-one-is-useless-in-this-world-who-lightens-the.

With the discovery of tea leaves in the Brahmaputra valley, in northeast India, by Scotsman Robert Bruce in 1823, cultivation of tea started during the British period. Tea leaves from Assam were first sent to the United Kingdom in 1838. India's domination as the number one tea producer continued for over a hundred years until China overtook it in 2005. Unfortunately, in recent times, the tea industry has crumbled, resulting in the laying off of lakhs of labourers in India.

The thriving tea industry has been reduced to one riddled with all sorts of problems. Issues include financial crises, power problems, labour problems, poor labour schemes, inadequate communication system, increased revenue tax for tea gardens, increased pollution fees, low transport subsidy, and so on. The age-old tea estates have been in trouble since the early 2000s. In recent years, some prestigious tea gardens have fallen sick, and some have even been closed down, rendering almost three lakh tea workers jobless and on the verge of starvation.

A tea garden labourer himself, Karimul has seen people struggle to make ends meet in the Dooars region of West Bengal. Between 2000 and 2015, more than 1400 people died in this region alone; most of the deaths were likely due to malnutrition after the loss of their livelihoods. According to Karimul, the number was possibly higher because many deaths had not been reported. The government proved unable to provide alternative jobs for these tea garden labourers.

If we look at the history of this industry, which is more than 150 years old, the condition of labourers has never been good. Most of them worked as part-timers and were mainly employed as per the production and requirements of the tea gardens during peak seasons. Though there were some 'permanent' workers who worked in the factories and offices, most of the labourers—third- or fourth-generation Adivasi migrants from Uttar Pradesh, Bihar, Jharkhand, Chhattisgarh or Madhya Pradesh—had been suffering from the very beginning. The tea workers generally stayed inside the tea garden; with no job opportunities outside, it was an enslavement of sorts for generations for them. During the peak season, tea gardens employed temporary labourers who were paid much lower than the minimum wage. Consequently, labourers lived under unhygienic conditions in the tea gardens. Moreover, with their meagre income, they could not educate their children who remained illiterate and fit only for labour work.

The labourers suffered the most in the field of healthcare. With illiteracy running high among them, there was little awareness about basic health practices, and personal and community hygiene. Communicable diseases due to lack of hygiene and sanitation and poor living conditions were rampant: these included worm infestation, respiratory problems, diarrhoea, skin infections, filariasis and pulmonary tuberculosis, to name a few. Emaciation among adults, micronutrient deficiency disorders like anaemia, and under-nutrition in children—which meant underweight children—were other health concerns that plagued them, along with hypertension, epilepsy and back pain. Fondness for alcohol and tobacco added to the woes of the Adivasi labourers in the form of liver cirrhosis and lung problems.

According to the Plantations Labour Act, 1951, every garden must provide a medical centre with proper facilities; this was something all the big tea estates had maintained in their heyday. But as tea gardens started incurring losses, the facilities went down, making the lives of the labourers very tough. Since most tea gardens are located in remote areas, it becomes difficult for workers to access health centres. Female workers have it even worse. They have no maternity benefits, and have to work during their pregnancy and the post-natal period, which adversely affects their health. Post-natal deaths and child mortality rates are also very high in these areas.

After tea estates closed down, in addition to healthcare issues, social evils came to the forefront, human trafficking perhaps being the worst of them. Hundreds of girls go missing from this area, but only two out of ten cases are reported. With poverty at home, these girls are lured with false promises of a better life, but ultimately fall into the clutches of traffickers. Once they leave home, they are untraceable.

Moved by their plight, Karimul got down to doing what he could for these former labourers and their families who were leading pitiable lives with their livelihoods gone. Ever since the early 2000s, Karimul has been conducting health camps and clothes distribution camps in various defunct tea gardens for the unemployed labourers and their families. Whenever people donate clothes, new or old, especially before Durga Puja, he organizes camps in the tea gardens and distributes the clothes. The health camps are especially focused on the old and needy tea garden workers. Deeply concerned about the reports of young women being trafficked, Karimul has taken up these issues with different government agencies on various occasions and at various times; he even reached out to Rajnath Singh, who was the union home minister at the time.

20

Family Matters

The only rock I know that stays steady, the only institution I know that works, is the family.

—Lee Iacocca[1]

A supportive family or a stable and dependable support system is essential for a man to succeed in life. Even as a child, Karimul was always blessed to have this support. His mother and elder brother stood rock solid in his childhood despite their poverty. As a loving and respectful son, Karimul always wanted the well-being of his mother, whose death without treatment completely changed his life. Khalilur has always been by his side, taking care of

---

[1] https://www.brainyquote.com/quotes/lee_iacocca_138664.

all his brothers and sisters like his own children. He had wanted Karimul to go to school regularly and complete his studies, regardless of their daily struggle for survival. When Karimul had broken his leg in a motorbike accident and was bedridden for six months, it was Khalilur who had taken care of the family with his meagre income. When Karimul started his bike ambulance service, his elder brother had encouraged him to carry on.

But Karimul's biggest strength has been his wife, Anjuwara Begum, who has supported, and even assisted, him in his journey as a saviour of many people's lives. She faced hardships in running the family but never complained. When her husband started his free bike service, she did not set up any obstacles, even though she knew it would take Karimul away from the family often. Rather, she whole-heartedly supported his cause.

There were days when Karimul had to take a patient who had no one to attend to him/her, and would take Anjuwara along as the attendant. One day, Karimul had come across a mentally disabled woman in Kranti Bazaar, who was seriously ill. He ferried the woman to the hospital, accompanied by Anjuwara. Since the patient had no one to take care of her, Anjuwara stayed with her as an attendant for four days. After she was discharged from hospital, Anjuwara and Karimul brought the woman to their home. She stayed with the Hak family for ten more days, and it was only after her complete recovery that the husband–wife duo allowed her to go. There have been numerous instances like this when Anjuwara has accompanied Karimul to the hospital with patients.

Likewise, she has never complained when Karimul has had to rush in the dead of the night to take patients to hospitals. Even on days when she found it difficult to wake up, especially after a tiring day, or when she was not well, she would help him get ready so that he could reach the patient's house promptly. She never expressed her fears for her husband's life, for the dangers he had to encounter when he ferried patients past the forest road; she knew he had to do what he had set out to do, and did not impose her worries on him.

She also helped her husband in running their home clinic. Be it measuring the blood pressure or administering saline to patients when they came to their home, Anjuwara was always there. When Karimul had to stitch up an open wound on a patient injured in an accident, she would keep all that he needed ready. Since Karimul would be preoccupied with his job in the tea garden or in ferrying or treating patients, or in blood donation camps, the wise Anjuwara never once burdened him with household issues, managing it all by herself.

There were days when Anjuwara and their children had to sleep on an empty stomach, but she never came in the way of her husband's mission of serving the poor. Karimul has, over the years, gratefully acknowledged that he was able to do his social work only because of his supportive wife. Anjuwara is happy with whatever they have; she never asks her husband for anything. She is content that she has been able to help her husband in keeping his promise to his late mother: that no one would die due to lack of medical treatment.

As they say, 'Like father like son'. Karimul's two sons—Raju and Rajesh—have also devoted their lives to the cause upheld by their father. Raju and Rajesh are both married now. While Raju has a son and a daughter, five-year-old Farhan and six-month-old Ayesha, Rajesh has a son, Saiyan, who is three years old. Initially, they used to run small shops in Kranti Bazaar, apart from helping their father in his work for the poor. There have been situations when Karimul got a call to help a patient even as he was tending to a patient at that very moment. He would then ask one of his sons to take care of the second patient—and they would do as told. Like their father, they are compassionate and have unhesitatingly pitched in to help others. Since their wives, Chhabina Begum and Sabina Begum, are as supportive as Anjuwara, they have been able to contribute to their father's cause.

But their lives took a 180-degree turn after their father received the Padma Shri. Since Karimul started putting in longer hours, they decided to close down their shops and support their father full-time. Raju is a fast thinker, a good communicator and organizer, and is tipped to carry forward Karimul's legacy. He supervises his father's projects. He also works as Karimul's personal secretary, attending to his phone calls and maintaining his events' diary. When his father is away for events and programmes, Raju carries out his social work, including his free bike ambulance service and the home clinic.

He also keeps an eye on his father's initiatives involving the differently abled. Raju hopes that once they complete the hospital, it will bring relief to the residents of the area. He is keen to have their hospital fitted with all diagnostic test facilities, such as ultrasonography and X-ray, so that villagers don't have to travel too far for treatment. Though he is not very educated, Raju wants his children to have a good education and also dreams of opening proper schools for poor children in villages.

Karimul's younger son, Rajesh, is a little shy. Unlike his elder brother, he likes to keep to himself but is a silent worker. These days, Rajesh has to look after many things, including the home clinic, since both his father and elder brother remain busy with other activities.

Noor Hossain, Karimul's stepbrother, too has supported him. When Karimul wanted to build his hospital near his home, he approached Noor with a request: if Noor and Karimul could exchange their plots of land, Karimul would be able to build his hospital close to his house. Noor willingly accepted the offer and exchanged his land with Karimul's. Karimul could not have started the work of the hospital had Noor not understood the reason behind Karimul's request and cooperated with him.

21

The Inspirations behind the Inspiration

People will forget what you said, people will forget what you did, but people will never forget how you made them feel.

—Maya Angelou[1]

Karimul Hak now inspires people. His bike ambulance service has become the talk of the town, perhaps even the nation. He is a hero for lakhs of the helpless poor. Undeterred by his own problems, he has soldiered on with single-minded focus to serve the poor with his free bike ambulance service. But the making of Karimul Hak

---

[1] https://www.goodreads.com/quotes/5934-i-ve-learned-that-people-will-forget-what-you-said-people.

would not have been possible without the inspiration and encouragement of some notable people.

If his mother was the biggest inspiration for him, the words and life of Swami Vivekananda also helped him serve the needy. As mentioned, Vivekananda's 'Jibe prem kore jei jon, sei jon sebiche Ishwar' has been the core of his life philosophy.

After returning from Bangladesh, the teenaged Karimul had attended a seminar on Vivekananda and been immediately attracted to this monk whose famous speech at Chicago had compelled the whole world to take note of India's vision of religion and humanity. Yet, he has not read any of Swami Vivekananda's books, nor any books on him. For that matter, Karimul has never read a book, as he is not comfortable with reading. But whatever he heard during that lecture on Swamiji changed his vision of life and its tenor.

We, the so-called learned people, read so many inspirational books or quotes. Our social media feeds are full of inspiring quotes, stories and films, which we see and share but rarely incorporate in our lives. Karimul has never read about inspirational characters, never watched a motivational movie. He has, instead, seen people struggle without basic healthcare, without basic education, without shelter and without clothes. But unlike so many people, he did not accept it as something that 'can't be changed'.

He did whatever he could to relieve people of their sufferings and pains. That's how he started his 24/7 free bike ambulance service. And as soon as he started this service, many people rallied around him, inspired him to continue.

When he took patients to Uttar Saripakuri Rural Health Centre, he would meet Dr Khiten Barman, the medical officer at the hospital. Karimul used to come to him with patients almost every day. Dr Barman, a benevolent man, never refused any patient. So, every time Karimul came to the hospital, he was never turned away. Besides, Dr Barman was very impressed by Karimul's energy and dedication. He had asked Karimul one day to spare a moment and sit with him. He wanted to know the reason behind Karimul ferrying patients. He also wanted to know the financial gains involved in this work. When Karimul told him that he provided free service to people, Dr Barman was overwhelmed. Then Karimul narrated the story of his mother's death.

Dr Barman was moved. He had never met such a generous person, so dedicated to working for the poor. He encouraged Karimul to continue his good work and assured him that he would extend a helping hand for the cause.

Karimul, in turn, was very inspired by Dr Barman, whose selfless service for the poor people of the region was an example for many doctors. Dr Barman seemed to live only for his patients. Sometimes, Karimul used to hesitate to disturb Dr Barman at odd hours; but he told Karimul not to think like that because, as a medical practitioner, it was his duty to serve people. Dr Barman never thought he was doing anything extraordinary. At a time when many doctors are focused on augmenting their bank balances rather than healing the sick and injured, people like Dr Barman give us hope.

Seeing Karimul come to the hospital virtually every day with patients, Dr Barman felt that Karimul should know some basic medical treatment. Therefore, whenever Karimul came with a patient, Dr Barman would explain in detail the symptoms of a particular disease or discuss in layman's terms the specifics of the case. Sometimes, he would even ask Karimul to make the diagnosis.

Dr Barman also taught him how to check blood pressure, blood sugar, use a thermometer, etc. Under his guidance, Karimul became a kind of 'doctor' who could understand and treat basic illnesses such as fever, cough, a running nose, an upset stomach, diarrhoea, etc. Dr Barman also taught Karimul how to administer saline to patients when they had severe diarrhoea and were dehydrated. He would pass on to Karimul the free sample medicines that medical representatives would give him, to help the poor patients of his area.

Karimul still holds Dr Barman close to his heart. Whenever Karimul would approach him, Dr Barman would always ask him whether he had had lunch or dinner. He would inquire about his wife, children and other family members. Dr Barman had, many a time, given Karimul money to buy something to eat. He often advised Karimul, too, on various matters. Whenever Karimul faced any kind of trouble, or was in a dilemma, he would turn to Dr Barman, as Karimul believed that he would never misguide him. Dr Barman was a charming personality and had a very good sense of humour. He often told Karimul that a day would come when the whole country would know of him and his free bike ambulance service.

It is an irony that he died just an hour before Karimul's name was announced for the Padma Shri, something that continues to haunt Karimul, just like his mother's death. Karimul Hak would not have become the man he is today had Dr Barman not understood his capabilities and shaped his indomitable spirit.

Another person who has been an inspirational figure for Karimul is Dr Soumen Mondal, a surgeon at Jalpaiguri Sadar Hospital. Whenever he went there with an accident case, he would meet Dr Mondal. Like Dr Barman, he admires and respects Karimul, and always encourages him to continue his noble work. Even if Karimul goes to his private chamber, he never charges a fee for Karimul's patients. He also donates medicines to Karimul's home clinic.

Like Dr Barman, Dr Mondal has taught Karimul a few basic medical aspects, such as how to stitch a minor injury, how to handle infections resulting from boils and how to detect the stomach pains originating from gallbladder stones or kidney stones. These days, Dr Mondal asks Karimul to identify the reason behind the pain, and then to match it with the ultrasound report.

There was a senior nurse in the hospital who would give Karimul Rs 100 whenever he met her in the hospital. Then there is Dr Nitai Mukherjee, a gynaecologist, who taught him how to take care of pregnant women. He also encouraged Karimul to continue his social work and never charged consultation fees from the patients Karimul brought in. Dr Rajat Bhattacharya and Dr Sumanta Mukherjee are other angels in white who help him whenever he goes to them with patients.

But it is Dr Khiten Barman whom Karimul feels most inspired by, amongst the doctors. At a time when many people are extending a helping hand to him and many avenues are opening up for him to work for the poor, Karimul feels Dr Barman's absence keenly.

22

A Social Entrepreneur

Whatever the mind can conceive and believe, it can achieve.

—Napoleon Hill[1]

Going by how Karimul Hak started his free bike ambulance service and solved the problem of the lack of ambulance facilities in many villages of his area, we can easily call him a social entrepreneur. Social entrepreneurs are those who have innovative ideas to solve pressing social problems. They create products, systems and solutions to help change people's lives. They have the passion and drive to go after solutions and the ability to take on risks. They are basically the change agents of society.

---

[1] https://en.wikiquote.org/wiki/Napoleon_Hill.

Look at the example of a social entrepreneur from Bangladesh, Muhammad Yunus, who was a co-awardee of the Nobel Peace Prize in 2006, with Grameen Bank, for pioneering the concept of microcredit and microfinance. He has had a tremendous impact on the lives of the poor people of Bangladesh. The international community has also supported and encouraged social entrepreneurs because they are keen to see such products or services go beyond geographical barriers.

With his free bike ambulance service, Karimul developed a model which provided a solution to a fundamental problem in his remote village. Before he started this service, hundreds of people died because of the unavailability of ambulances. But the scenario changed once Karimul started his bike ambulance service. Not only his village, but people from other villages too have benefited from it. Karimul now wants this service to be taken up in every corner of the country, and even beyond it.

There are still many parts of India where the roads are such that a standard four-wheeled ambulance cannot run on them, but a motorbike can easily go there. So, a bike ambulance is more effective in such areas. Apart from that, the bike ambulance is very cost-effective as it consumes far less fuel compared to the conventional ambulance.

Though the idea of a bike ambulance is not a new concept, Karimul made it popular. And it became even more popular when he was awarded the Padma Shri. India's defence ministry sought Karimul's help to know whether it could be used to evacuate wounded soldiers from remote areas, instead of sending a regular ambulance.

To seek Karimul's expertise, Divakar Sharma, incharge, technical coordination and project management of Defence Research and Development Organization (DRDO), visited his home in June 2018 and learned about the nuances of his bike ambulance service. Karimul gave him several ideas regarding this service and how it could be used by the army to save the lives of soldiers. He suggested fitting bikes with life-saving oxygen cylinders and saline bottles for emergency evacuations. He stressed the fact that the bike ambulance could be the difference between life and death, as it saves precious time for critically injured patients, compared to four-wheelers, in the absence of proper roads.

For Divakar Sharma, it was not merely the technical session with Karimul that was useful; the visit to Karimul's house was hugely inspirational too. He was moved by Karimul's selfless work and journey. For him, all the education we get, all the technical knowledge we acquire, is useless if we don't use it for the service of the poor. In that sense, Sharma opined, Karimul is one of the most educated people he has ever met.

In November 2018, the Central Reserve Police Force (CRPF), with the help of DRDO's Institute of Nuclear Medicine & Allied Sciences (INMAS), finally developed a motorcycle ambulance. It has a special pillion seat that has support for the spine and neck, and a saline stand, along with provision for carrying medicines and injections. Dozens of such bikes have been produced. These bikes will initially be deployed in camps across Left-Wing Extremism (LWE)-hit areas in Chhattisgarh, with preference being given to remote and inaccessible locations.

Evacuation is challenging in areas like Bastar due to the terrain. In these areas, there are either no roads or there are non-metal roads that may have mines. In these circumstances, bikes eliminate the risk of being caught in an IED explosion. These bikes will be also utilized for civic action programmes such as ferrying sick tribals to the nearest medical facilities in Chhattisgarh.

In Jharkhand, too, the CRPF has launched the indigenously designed bike ambulance service to provide health facilities to people in the interior areas of Latehar district.

Another bike ambulance service was recently launched at the Matlong Campo of 133 Battalion of the CRPF.[2]

---

[2] https://indianexpress.com/article/india/bike-ambulances-to-special-shoes-drdo-arms-crpf-for-maoist-areas-5346841/.

A foldable canopy with a backrest, hand rest and seat extension for patients are the main features of these bikes. The bikes also have wheel guards on both sides, along with a footrest with grip, first-aid box, a beacon light and a hooter.

Earlier, the bike ambulance was seen mostly in the cities in India. It was first introduced in Karnataka in 2015 to provide critical medical support to patients in need till the four-wheeled ambulance arrived. This was primarily a trauma care initiative termed the 'platinum 10 minutes'. Named the 'Arogya Kavacha' ambulance service, the bikes are equipped with forty emergency-care medical items such as stethoscope, pulse oxymeter, bandages and IV normal saline, apart from fifty-three basic drugs. The bike ambulance was then introduced in Mumbai (2017) and Chandigarh (2018). The drivers of the bike ambulance are trained paramedics; they reach the patients within ten minutes and provide basic healthcare services.

23

Another Feather in His Cap

If you can dream it, you can do it.

—Walt Disney[1]

When the Almighty shines the spotlight on a simple person, the world stands up to honour him or her. People admire these individuals for finding a solution to an enormous problem, for considering the dignity of humanity at large, for acting selflessly, putting others before their own needs—and for not giving up, come what may. But the recognition comes after several years of toil, sweat and tears, and, even then, only to a few.

---

[1] https://www.goodreads.com/quotes/24673-if-you-can-dream-it-you-can-do-it-always.

So it has been with Karimul. He neither craved awards nor expected anything in return for his free bike ambulance service. In fact, he had never even heard of the Padma Shri and what it stood for. He learnt of its significance and the respect it commands much later.

When the Government of India conferred the Padma Shri on him, Karimul shot to fame. Yet, he remains very humble and down-to-earth, and is only interested in the upliftment of the poor, helpless and vulnerable people of his region. So, when he was invited to speak at a TEDx Talk, he brushed it aside, thinking it to be a waste of time. The organizers called him again and explained the importance of the TEDx programme; Karimul then consulted his well-wishers. On learning that giving a TEDx Talk is an honour and a privilege, that it is a huge platform for sharing one's views, and that only those who have worked to effect a change in society are asked to deliver a speech, Karimul acquiesced; he would speak at the upcoming TEDx event.

The event was organized by TEDx Youth@ DarjeelingMore, at a private management college in Siliguri, on 8 October 2018. Since TEDx talks are aired, some well-wishers advised him to prepare a speech beforehand and rehearse it well, as it would be viewed by millions of people around the world. But Karimul believes that speaking from the heart is better than giving a scripted speech; he speaks what he believes. Moreover, since he had often been invited to speak at various programmes after the Padma Shri, his oratorical skills had improved in leaps and bounds! He may not be our typical, sophisticated, motivational speaker, but people love to listen to him as there is no hypocrisy in what he says. His speeches in ordinary language help him establish a deep bond with the audience.

Karimul Hak was given eighteen minutes to speak. He spoke in Hindi, a language he was comfortable with. Since a large part of the audience was made up of students, he focused on the student community. Introducing himself as the 'Bike Ambulance Dada', Karimul said that he could see future district magistrates (DMs), superintendents of police (SPs), deputy superintendents of police (DSPs), ministers sitting there, in front of him. He told them he was an ordinary man who was just performing his duty towards his mother, and he shared the story behind his free bike ambulance and basic healthcare services.

He candidly rued neglecting his studies when he was young, failing to realize its importance. As a result, he now feels severely handicapped because, among other things, he is unable to communicate with many people—especially those from outside India—as he doesn't know English. He emphasized the importance of education in life, as educated people are respected everywhere, irrespective of their caste, creed and religion. At the same time, one must also be compassionate and large-hearted; backed by good education, one can accomplish great things, he told his rapt audience.

Karimul also expressed his concern about the current education system that seemed to be producing mostly selfish students—students who attacked their principals or teachers. Expressing deep anguish, Karimul said that such activities needed to stop and asked the students to be respectful to their teachers. While speaking about respect, Karimul included within its ambit respect towards parents, teachers and women. 'If any woman anywhere is insulted, you should feel that your mother is getting insulted—we are in this world because of our mothers,' he said.

Karimul also urged them to help the needy. 'This should be your goal in life, this should be your mission. This is your religion,' he exhorted the students who applauded his every word.

He reminded them that only two things are constant in life—birth and death—which are unavoidable. In between, we should work for the betterment of needy people; we will all die one day and bid adieu to earthly pleasures, but before that we have to do something which will immortalize us. Quoting Vivekananda, Karimul said one should create a lasting impressing on the minds of people by doing something good before one's death.

Karimul pointed out that if he, an 'uneducated' man, could get the Padma Shri, each and every one present there, in the audience, was capable of getting one too; in fact, they had the talent to be awarded higher civilian awards such as the Padma Bhushan, Padma Vibhushan, or even the Bharat Ratna. He also informed the audience that his biopic was in the pipeline and his official biography would be published soon. He declared that whatever money he got from the film and the book would be spent on welfare activities, including weddings of girls from poor families.

He said he worked as a peon, as he had nothing to offer to anyone. Well-off people donate things to the poor; his role was to work as a courier, delivering those things to the needy. He himself wore what others had given him, including his attire on that very day. He gestured at his wristwatch which, he said, was given to him a few years ago by the then north Bengal development minister, Gautam Deb.

After the event, the spellbound students surrounded Karimul to take selfies with him.

24

Politics over Karimul

Politics determine who has the power, not who has the truth.

—Paul Krugman[1]

The political space of Bengal has undergone a sea change. The degradation of the state's political culture is now a very disturbing phenomenon. There is tension everywhere over politics in Bengal, with the situation in rural Bengal being the worst. West Bengal, once a model state for education and culture, has earned a bad name because of political violence which has been the cause of many a death in the state.

---

[1] https://www.goodreads.com/quotes/293460-politics-determines-who-has-the-power-not-who-has-the.

Karimul has seen the political culture changing in West Bengal before his very eyes. The degradation in Bengal's socio-political life started in the early 2000s under the left front rule, whose leaders were very proud of their honesty and integrity in public life. But the old adage, 'Power corrupts and absolute power corrupts absolutely', came to haunt the communist leaders.

Corruption, however, did not touch the top leadership. There were exceptions, but most of the top leaders were known for their simple lifestyle. Leaders like former chief ministers Jyoti Basu and Buddhadeb Bhattacharjee led a common man's lifestyle. However, problems cropped up in rural Bengal where many leaders had fallen into the trap of being in power for too long. The uninterrupted thirty-four-year rule had made the leaders very arrogant as well. The party had become too big a persona, leaving its mark on everything in Bengal's social, political and even cultural lives.

With the lack of employment opportunities, the populace had become dependent on politics and political parties. One could avail of nothing without the patronage of political parties and political leaders. The rural people, the poor and downtrodden, had become akin to slaves of the left parties. Nowhere else in India would you see such dependence on a political system in rural areas or panchayat levels, as you would in West Bengal. If you were not a party member, you would be deprived of any kind of welfare schemes for the poor. Even if you were very poor, you would not find your name in the BPL (Below Poverty Line) list, which determines your 'fate' to be eligible for the welfare schemes. Naturally, people in the rural areas became hugely dependent on politics which were largely controlled by the left government till 2011, until the Trinamool Congress (TMC), led by Mamata Banerjee, finally ousted the left rulers.

Ground-level netas of the left party had become corrupt. The lifestyle of some leaders was questionable. The culture of political violence started from the early 2000s. Winning by any means became the mantra of the government. Anti-social elements sheltered by the government ruled the roost. Rampant rigging during elections was the norm of the times, and they clung to power in the last ten years of their rule only by ensuring total party control over the government.

Health and education were two areas where the situation remained very grim under left rule. Karimul fought for improvement in these two areas. Had there been an ambulance in the vicinity, he could have taken his mother to hospital, and later his daughter. In most rural health centres, there were no doctors or nurses. The left government did little to improve the health sector in West Bengal. Fed up with the pathetic state of affairs in his part of West Bengal, Karimul took the onus on himself to serve the people of his village and adjoining villages. His selfless single-handed effort in taking critically ill patients to the nearest hospitals saved countless lives.

The other neglected area, as mentioned earlier, was the education sector. With the English language ousted from primary school education, and with most school teachers becoming active party members, the quality of education took a severe beating. Karimul could not get proper education due to poverty and the lack of opportunity. The same happened to his sons and daughters who could not study beyond Class X. This meant that in the years between Karimul's childhood and that of his children there was no appreciable development in education opportunities in rural areas. Job opportunities too lagged behind. The number of educated and uneducated unemployed youth increased manifold.

Karimul was also becoming frustrated at the overall scenario in Bengal in the early 2000s. Despite being poor, he did his best to help people out through his bike ambulance service and his home and mobile dispensary services. But it pained him to see how the people's representatives—the panchayat, the pradhan, MLAs, MPs and ministers—remained indifferent to the problems encountered by those who had voted them to power. The netas and minsters only knew lip service.

People of Bengal were unhappy with the political scenario. Around 2006, when Karimul was seriously thinking of purchasing a bike and providing a free bike ambulance service, the citizens of Bengal were also preparing for a change in government. Bengal started to burn over the issue of land given to the Tata Group for their upcoming Tata Nano project in Hoogly's Singur.

The left government, led by the CPI (M), which had once protested against farmlands being used for tea gardens or industrial purposes, had to change its stand due to the rapid increase of population and lack of employment options. With West Bengal lagging behind other states in terms of key indicators like poverty rate, infant mortality rate, job growth rate, per capita income, the then government, under the progressive chief minister Buddhadeb Bhattacharya, had no option but to go for rapid industrialization to catch up with other states.

Though several states were keen on getting the Tata Nano project, the cheapest car in the world, the Tata Group chose West Bengal. But right from the beginning, there were plenty of controversies with the government forcing people to evacuate the proposed lands. The compensation they were offered was not satisfactory and the new housing facilities offered by Tata were delayed. The peasants started to protest. For the main Opposition leader in the state, Mamata Banerjee, who was fighting to end the left rule, it was a shot in the arm. She at once jumped on the bandwagon in favour of the peasants, giving a new lease of life to their movement.

This movement helped Mamata Banerjee grab power in Bengal in 2011, but at the ground level, the situation did not change much. Like the majority of people, Karimul also expected a real *poribartan* (change) when Banerjee took over the reins of Bengal. She started off well, giving importance to healthcare, education, roads and infrastructure. Her image as an honest politician also gave new hope to people who were frustrated with corruption.

But things hardly changed at the ground level. Allegations of corruption continued to surface, leaving the people more frustrated. The TMC understood that people had started to get disenchanted with their governance. People of the northern part of Bengal, where Karimul lived, were the most dissatisfied. So the TMC vied for Karimul's support with their main political rivals currently, the Bharatiya Janata Party (BJP). Before the 2019 Lok Sabha elections, Karimul was at the centre of a tug of war between the BJP and the TMC, with both parties trying hard to win his support. A popular personality in the region, especially among the youth, Karimul's support would have encouraged the youth to vote for the party he supported. The Mamata-led TMC got a rude shock in the 2019 general elections after losing eighteen seats in Bengal.

Almost all the seats in the northern region were captured by the BJP.

Ever since Karimul Hak was awarded the Padma Shri by the then NDA government led by Narendra Modi, the political circle believed him to be close to the BJP. The BJP leaders and central ministers frequently visited his house, and this only served to add credibility to what the TMC leaders already believed—that he was close to the central government. Despite achieving so much, he generates hardly any euphoria in the TMC top brass. Karimul sometimes regrets not being given any award by the state government.

Karimul, a secular Muslim who also recites Hindu shlokas, seems to fit the bill for the BJP. However, he has always maintained a safe distance from politics. In his opinion, everyone respects and admires him immensely, but if he supports any political party, he will lose the trust reposed in him. He wants to serve the poor only through his social work and wishes to remain one of them. Joining politics, he believes, will come in the way of his charitable work for the poor.

As a social reformer, Karimul is disheartened to see Bengal politics headed in the wrong direction and the youth being used for political violence by different parties. He is haunted by a simple question: Why does even a single person have to die in elections? This was not the intention of our great leaders when they fought for the country's independence. He wants the youth to be fruitfully engaged and employed. Unfortunately, he opines, nobody is bothered about that right now.

Fully aware of the potential that students possess, he wants them to come forward and help others; it is the students and youth who can stop corruption in society, he says. He is hopeful that people will understand the dirty tricks of the politicians and select good people to run the government.

25

Concept of an Ideal Village

Let new India arise out of the peasant's cottage, grasping the
plough, out of huts, cobbler and sweeper.

—Swami Vivekananda[1]

With 70 per cent of Indians residing in villages, the
country's progress depends on the development of rural
India. Realizing the need to improve the condition of
villages, Mahatma Gandhi had famously declared: 'The
soul of India lives in its villages.' If rural India improves
its health, India will also be healthy. With urban India
becoming unliveable by the day, Karimul wants the

---

[1] *India's Freedom Movement: Legacy of Bipin Chandra Pal*, Binay
Bhattacharya, ebook, p. 115.

government to focus on improving the socioeconomic condition of the villages, so that fewer people think of migrating to the big cities.

Karimul dreams of a day when educated people, who had left their homes for better opportunities in the metro cities, return to their villages. To turn this dream into a reality, Karimul is currently working hard to develop Rajadanga as a model village and come up with a concept that can inspire other villages in India to follow this example.

In his concept of an ideal village, he has pointed out some areas that need focus. He considers health, education, sanitation, economy and employability, and drinking water to be the key aspects that should be improved to make the perfect—or near-perfect—village.

*

As Karimul started working in the health sector first, by providing the bike ambulance service, setting up a clinic at his home and organizing health camps at different places, healthcare remains the core area in his ideal village concept. He believes that every human being has the right to reliable and timely medical facilities.

If there is no medical facility in a village, the inhabitants will never be able to stay healthy. In India, there are innumerable villages where there is neither a doctor nor an ambulance facility. Apart from that, a vast majority of the Indian population does not have access to basic medicines and medical facilities. Many people die because they are deprived of basic healthcare. Most deaths occur in the rural areas where there is rarely any prenatal and postnatal care.

Karimul wants to improve the health scenario in villages by ensuring at least one permanent doctor and a nurse in each village hospital or medical centre, so that people have access to 24/7 medical facilities in the village itself. He also wants at least one ambulance in every village so that critically ill patients can be ferried to the nearest district hospital or medical college as soon as possible.

Because of the lack of facilities offered by the public sector, people are forced to turn to private hospitals. As there is no government regulation, private medical services have become very expensive in India. So rural people belonging to the low-income group end up losing almost all of the little they own after treatment in private hospitals.

Karimul urges corporate hospital chains to come up with low-cost medical solutions for poor people. He believes that the time has come for corporate hospitals to improve their image with low-cost options. With the help of well-wishers, he is in the process of developing a proper hospital adjacent to his house, where the villagers will get proper medical facilities either at very minimal rates or free of cost. He has asked the government to concentrate on the healthcare sector and work towards improving the health of the people. If the health sector does not improve in rural regions, people will continue to migrate to cities, which are already bursting at the seams.

*

Along with health, another important feature of an ideal village is an adequate education set-up. Despite getting independence almost seventy years ago, it's unfortunate that we still lag behind in this important indicator of human development: education. Like health, village education is in a shambles in most parts of the country.

A report[2] suggests that half of the students in Class V at government schools are unable to read the textbooks of Class II. Nor can they solve the mathematical problems of Class II. Though student enrolment has increased in rural areas, the quality of education has not improved; in some states the attendance of teachers and students is also declining. Apart from that, there are problems such as lack of committed teachers, good textbooks and teaching/

---

[2] '50% Class 5 students cannot read text of Class 2 level: 10 highlights from ASER Education Report 2018', *India Today*, 16 January 2019.

learning aides. Compared to private schools, the quality of government schools leaves much to be desired.

Karimul is now concentrating on improving the quality of education in the villages in and around his own. He believes the villagers can change their fortunes only by providing proper education to their children. To take correct decisions in life, proper education is a necessity. Moreover, if people become truly educated, there will be fewer chances of electing corrupt representatives. Once educated, citizens will also become more conscious about health. According to Karimul, education is the backbone of the society and the only way to create ideal citizens. After all, we can build an ideal village with model citizens only.

He has already opened a few one-teacher schools that concentrate on basic pre-primary and primary education. He hopes that every child gets the opportunity to go to school and that there are no drop-outs. To this end, Karimul arranges meetings with the guardians and sensitizes them about the importance of education in their children's lives.

He hopes that there will be a day when every village has at least one school. He has repeatedly urged the government to improve the condition of government schools and ensure quality of education.

*

If India has to improve, its villages have to improve. Indian villages contribute to 46 per cent of the total net product and 70 per cent of the total workforce.[3] Unless villages become economically self-reliant, unless the economy of the villages improves, India will not shine.

Since agriculture is the backbone of the Indian village economy, its upliftment is possible only by improving the agricultural sector and practices. Karimul wants the government to encourage rural people to take up agri-business seriously with the help of modern technology and modern facilities. Though India's last two budgets were pro-agriculture, a far-greater boost is needed to make Prime Minister Modi's vision of doubling of farmers' income by 2022 a reality.

Almost two-thirds of India's population lives in rural areas, most of them in abject poverty. The reason is that the rural population is largely dependent on agriculture, but this sector's productivity is inadequate compared to the global average. For productivity to improve, the country needs better irrigation facilities, technological improvement, diversifying towards higher value-added crops (like fruits, vegetables, spices, condiments), and increase in crop intensity.

---

[3] 'Changing Structure of Rural Economy of India: Implications for Employment and Growth', Ramesh Chand, S.K. Srivastava and Jaspal Singh, NITI Aayog, November 2017.

Moreover, according to Karimul, our farmers also need price realization. The government has to ensure that agriculture prices do not fall below minimum support prices (MSP). Karimul has time and again urged the government to start proper educational facilities and skill development programmes for farmers. He feels that a strong push is needed in the field of food processing, warehousing and logistics, which will also help increase income of the farmers, reduce the wastage of perishable agriculture commodities and provide employment to rural workers.

But Karimul wants people to concentrate on non-agriculture sectors as well in order to transform rural economy and rural employability. He is keen on providing appropriate skill training to the rural workforce to enable them to get absorbed in the non-agriculture sectors.

*

In many Indian villages, high levels of arsenic in the groundwater affect people. Unlike other water problems such as iron contamination, the presence of arsenic in water is not obvious in taste or appearance. It typically derives from natural deposits in the earth's crust and requires chemical, not biological, treatment. This natural deposit has slow but deadly consequences for humans, which include scaling and pigmentation of the skin, stomach pain, nausea, vomiting, diarrhoea, numbness of hands and feet, partial paralysis, blindness and other fatalities. Arsenic has also been linked to cancer of the bladder, lungs, skin, kidney, nasal passages, liver and prostate.

Many people consume arsenic-contaminated water without realizing it and grow to accept their slow health deterioration. The World Health Organization (WHO) has, therefore, deemed it a global public health problem.

Karimul feels that water is very important for the overall health of the villagers and children's growth. Without it, we can't build an ideal village in India. In association with the Tagore-Sengupta Foundation, Karimul is working to address drinking water problems in his village and an adjacent one. The Tagore-Sengupta Foundation has recently installed two water projects, one in Karimul's village and the other in the adjacent village where the quality of water was very poor.

The easy-to-operate units provide arsenic-safe drinking water using regenerable arsenic adsorbents, and can be started or stopped with no real-time lag. When the filter is exhausted, the adsorbent material is regenerated (unlike most filters, which are simply discarded) through a simple process consisting of a well-aerated coarse sand filter at a central location. This decreases the waste volume by cleaning the adsorbents of collected arsenic and catching the leftover arsenic sludge in the filter. The cleaned absorbent material is then returned to the water unit, filtering water as if the unit were new. This disposal technique, developed and validated under rural conditions, is scientifically more appropriate than dumping arsenic-loaded adsorbents into landfills, which is the typical practice in developed nations.

The lesson learned from arsenic mitigation projects in severely affected regions is the realization that in every crisis there is an opportunity for innovation and holistic growth. The use of shared, community-based water filtration systems has spurred individual innovation while providing clean water to a large number of people.

In West Bengal, 'one community's small tariff for filtered water has produced enough economic wealth that the village's water committee hired a full-time worker to maintain the unit. As the years passed and more money was collected, the committee elected to renovate the water distribution centre by placing the unit in a covered pavilion and displaying a television to provide entertainment to the community members waiting in line. The water council, doubling its revenue between 2005 and 2009, is now organizing a micro-finance operation to encourage further innovation in the community. The opportunity emerging from the arsenic crisis is community-centric, organic and local to their needs.'[4]

---

[4] tagoresenguptafoundation.weebly.com

26

Karimul's Life in Celluloid

It does not matter how slowly you go as long as you do not stop.

—Confucius[1]

Even though Karimul didn't have the luxury of watching films in movie halls, he is a film and music buff. He still remembers watching his first movie—in Bangladesh in a video hall. In those days, when a TV set was beyond the reach of ordinary people, one would go to video halls to watch movies. In the video halls of villages or small towns, there was no screen as such. The audience would watch a film that was played through a video cassette on the TV

---

[1] https://www.brainyquote.com/quotes/confucius_140908.

that was placed in the 'hall'. It was a big hit as villagers did not have any medium of 'modern' entertainment in those days. They would throng the village video halls in large numbers in the evening. Though Karimul has forgotten the name of the film he watched in Bangladesh, he remembers how thrilled he was at the time. Back in India, he watched some films in the Kranti video hall as films fascinated him.

The first film that he watched in the Kranti video hall was in the 1980s—*Sadhna*, a black-and-white movie that was produced in 1958. Directed by B.R. Chopra, the film starred Sunil Dutt and Vyjayanthimala. It revolved around the rehabilitation of a prostitute, a role beautifully played by Vyjayanthimala. The film had a deep impact on the sensitive Karimul. He became an ardent fan of the actress after watching that movie.

Thereafter, Karimul went on to watch movies of Amitabh Bachchan—*Sholay*, *Namak Halaal*, *Anand*, *Deewar*, *Amar Akbar Anthony*, *Coolie*—and with each movie, his admiration for the superstar grew. He was also a fan of Dharmendra. In *Sholay*, he claims to have liked Dharmendra's acting and role more than Bachchan's. Being a Bengali, he has always had a soft corner for Mithun Chakraborty. He saw Mithun's famous movie, *Disco Dancer*, which established the actor as one of the top Bollywood actors of that era. Among actresses, apart from Vyjayanthimala, he enjoyed watching films of Hema Malini, Meenakshi Seshadri and Padmini Kolhapure.

When director Vinay Mudgil, who was the assistant director of the popular Bollywood film *Hum Saath Saath Hain*, called Karimul in November 2017 to inform him that he was planning a biopic on him, Karimul couldn't believe his ears. He did not believe his life could be turned into a movie and kept Mudgil's request to himself, as he did not take it seriously. But a few days later, Karimul again got a call from Mudgil, who informed him that he and a few others would be visiting him in December. After they had fixed a mutually convenient date, Karimul spoke about the biopic and Mudgil to others, including his family and villagers.

As decided, Mudgil and his team arrived in Karimul's village in December 2017. They stayed at a resort in Gorumara National Park, close to his house. But what made Mudgil focus on Karimul?

Talking to reporters,[2] Mudgil said, 'Karimul can be an inspiration for many . . . this is one man who lives for others. Even with his meagre income, he tries and helps people. Not every day do we come across a person like him. I had a wonderful time interacting with his family there.

---

[2] https://timesofindia.indiatimes.com/city/kolkata/bolly-biopic-on-bengals-ambulance-man/articleshow/62373221.cms.

They are simple people with hearts of gold. We have signed an agreement and I have offered 50 per cent profit from the film to Karimul. I hope the money helps him in his cause.' Mudgil's assistant, Aloke Singh, said that while they had some actors in mind to play the lead role, they would approach them only when the script was ready.

Karimul is still very surprised by the prospect of a mainstream Bollywood movie based on his life. 'I do what I do with the belief that everyone in need of a doctor should be able to reach the hospital. The filmmakers have told me that they will come to visit me to take notes on what I do every day and how I lead my life. They will then take me to Mumbai to interact with the actor who is selected to play me,' he said.

27

Still a Long Way to Go

*Strong people stand up for themselves. The strongest people
stand up for others.*

—Chris Gardner[1]

Dream. Dream big. The first step to achieving something
in life is to dream.

When Karimul's mother died without treatment,
he dreamt of a day when nobody would die the way she
did—without treatment—in remote areas of the country.
Karimul has ensured this in his area. He has saved countless
lives so far through his free bike ambulance service. But

---

[1] https://quotecatalog.com/quote/chris-gardner-strong-people-s-
x1m9e41/.

several critical problems remain to be tackled in the healthcare sector in rural India—and these are the issues that Karimul wants to address soon.

Karimul looks forward to a day when all rural hospitals or health centres in the country are equipped with state-of-the-art facilities. In any emergency, these hospitals should swing into action to serve poor patients. Added to this, Karimul is also clear that the rural poor must get easy access to free medicines.

He praises Prime Minister Modi for launching Ayushman Bharat Yojana, a medical insurance scheme under which poor people will get a cover of Rs 5 lakh. Karimul believes that this scheme—slated to cover almost fifty crore citizens of India—will help the poor who often die without getting proper and timely medical treatment. He says that Ayushman Bharat Yojana is a step in the right direction.

There are many hospitals and health centres in rural areas which somehow 'function' without a doctor. Sadly, most doctors are not interested in working in villages. For Karimul, this is the outcome of our faulty education and social system, which encourages personal ambition rather than serving the society. He regrets the lack of selflessness and civic duty among students, or the young generation, who seem more concerned about their own material comforts and bank balance. Doctors, he said, should come forward and serve the poor. He would like the government to include value education in the education syllabus. He rues that there are not many inspirational people these days who can be role models for the young generation.

In addition to his free bike ambulance service, as mentioned earlier, Karimul also provides basic healthcare facilities at his house. These facilities are mostly availed by the needy in his village and the nearby villages.

After some thought, Karimul decided to build a hospital on his own farmland beside his house in Dhalabari village. He named his hospital Manab Seva Hospital (Humanity Hospital), through which he hopes to reach out to more people, especially those who can't afford basic healthcare. He started the construction of the hospital with the help of donations from a few people.

A woman from Siliguri had initially given him Rs 2 lakh in 2018, in the memory of her departed daughter. Some other people made cash donations. Karimul started the construction of the building with an initial amount of Rs 3 lakh but had to stop after the roof-casting of the ground floor because the funds dried up. But Karimul was not a man to be stopped by such a setback. He kept approaching people, and more help came his way.

The Tagore-Sengupta Foundation, which installed water plants in different areas of Karimul's village, donated some money and decided to build the guest house of the hospital. Apurba Ghosh, an electrical contractor in Siliguri, promised to do all the electrical work for free. A noted social worker of Jalpaiguri, Krishna Kumar Kalyani, gave him Rs 1 lakh. Another good soul, Kalyan Debnath, originally from Siliguri but now staying in New York, contributed Rs 1.5 lakh. Apart from these, many people and social organizations came up with small amounts of money—Rs 10,000 or 15,000—which went into helping him restart the construction of the hospital building after a year or so. Finally, the chairman of the Siliguri Jalpaiguri Development Authority (SJDA), Bijay Chandra Barman, allocated Rs 3 lakh to the hospital. With this, Karimul hopes to complete the ground floor of the building and throw open the doors soon.

He has talked to many famous doctors, too, such as Dr Devi Shetty, the noted heart surgeon, and Dr Nageshwar Reddy of Hyderabad, who have assured him that they will come over to treat patients at his hospital. Apart from this, numerous doctors from his region, who regularly organized health camps at his house and the villages with him, have also promised to start free clinics at his hospital. Karimul hopes that with their help, and that of the government, he can have a good hospital up and running—something that will be of immense benefit to the poor of north Bengal.

His plans also include an air-conditioned ambulance fitted with modern equipment, which will transport critical patients to Kolkata free of cost. To make this a reality, he has submitted proposals to a few social organizations; he is optimistic about starting this ambulance service very soon.

Another thing Karimul has been insisting upon for a long time is a bridge over the Chell river, which will reduce the distance to the nearest good government hospital by almost 30 kilometres, benefiting around 2.5 lakh people of this area. When former cabinet minister S.S. Ahluwalia had visited Karimul to congratulate him on his Padma Shri, Karimul had raised this issue—and once again when he had met Modi. Prime Minister Modi had assured him that the bridge would be constructed. He has made this demand to the state government as well. Karimul is certain that either the state government or the central government will have the bridge built over the Chell, and he will get to see it in his lifetime.

Ever since Karimul received the Padma Shri, the expectations of the poor have increased considerably. People not only seek his help for his free bike ambulance service, but also for solutions to other problems. He sees this as an opportunity to expand his work and dreams. Since both his sons, Raju and Rajesh, have taken over the responsibility of running the bike ambulance service, Karimul has started focusing on other areas, like primary education and vocational education.

He has already opened six donor schools in his village and some other villages with one lady teacher. Here, children who drop out of school are given primary education. One benefactor from Kolkata is financially supporting these schools. He plans to open more such schools where children can learn the fundamentals of math, English and Bengali, and can rejoin mainstream education. Quite a few village children have already benefited. With more funding, he plans to open more such schools in the coming days. Besides, a couple from Pune is helping him by bearing the educational costs of some high-school girl students.

He has a special plan for girls' education, especially vocational education for women. He has engaged both his daughters to teach sewing to the young women in the vicinity. Once they complete their training, he plans to donate a sewing machine to each of the girls. He has been toying with the idea of forming a group of women whom he will train in varied production work in small-scale industry.

Karimul, who cared deeply for his mother, is at a loss to understand why children neglect their parents and overlook their needs when they grow old. He is even more surprised when an educated man or woman neglects their parents—and he once again blames the education system for this. To rectify this oversight in the current education syllabus, Karimul is seriously pondering opening value education centres in different regions of north Bengal.

He is also worried about the quality of drinking water, not only in his area but also in other parts of the district. He thinks that the poor quality of drinking water is the main reason for so many diseases in rural areas. Recently, the Tagore-Sengupta Foundation, Pennsylvania, USA, and the Society for Technology with a Human Face, Kolkata, installed a huge water treatment plant in his home, from where many villagers take drinking water. Recently, they also installed two more plants in other villages with Karimul's help. He wants more such organizations to come forward and install water treatment plants in every village of the country, which will reduce the number of diseases caused by poor drinking water.

28

Life Now

If you are humble, nothing will touch you, neither praise nor disgrace, because you know what you are.

—Mother Teresa[1]

Before the Padma Shri, Karimul was known only in his village and the surrounding region. Transporting patients to hospitals on his bike ambulance, providing free basic healthcare service to the poor, arranging medical camps and blood donation camps, and working in the tea garden made up Karimul's daily life. But post the award, his popularity increased manifold, as did his area of work.

---

[1] https://www.goodreads.com/quotes/55677-if-you-are-humble-nothing-will-touch-you-neither-praise.

The biggest change is that now people have been reaching out to him, from different states of India, and even abroad. Earlier, he had to ask for money, but now help comes automatically or voluntarily.

Both organizations and individuals now come forward of their own accord to donate essentials of daily living and dry food items to Karimul, who passes these on to the needy. Karimul has now stepped into other sectors— educating poor children, be they girl students or drop-outs; generating employment by training girls of his area; and working for the disabled, as also elderly women. Of course, his work in the health sector of the region continues.

Nowadays, Karimul himself fixes appointments with noted doctors of the country if any poor patient needs major treatment or a surgery. If he refers any poor patient to the doctors or hospitals, they get free treatment. Besides, if anyone is in some other kind of trouble, Karimul knows a few well-placed government officials and ministers whom he can call to get justice for an innocent person. His fame helps him to carry out his service for the poor.

After his TEDx Talk and the news of his biopic in the making becoming known, Karimul received several more invitations to attend programmes in different parts of the state—and still does. He is also asked to inaugurate cultural programmes during religious festivals, be it Durga Puja, Kali Puja, Eid, Muharram or other celebrations.

It so happened that Karimul was once called to attend a hugely popular show on Zee TV, *Sa Re Ga Ma Pa*. On hearing his story, the participants, judges and others on the show couldn't hold back their tears. Neha Kakkar, one of the judges and a popular singer, declared she would donate Rs 1 lakh for his cause. Karimul's popularity increased further after the show.

During a Dussehra programme in 2018, Karimul addressed a gathering of 15,000 people. He had been invited there as the chief guest, to a place called Rajganj, some 25 kilometres from Siliguri. He spoke for fifteen minutes and the gathering cheered him on. After the event, he was mobbed by the people there, all clamouring for a selfie with him. This was despite the fact that the local MP, MLA and many other dignitaries were present there. Naturally, many organizations now want him as a chief guest, as he has become a crowd-puller.

Wherever Karimul goes, he becomes an instant hit with the audience. The message he delivers is simple yet profound. Karimul urges them to respect their parents, realize the importance of education—reiterating that he still faces difficulties because he neglected his studies—and serve the poor, and for the last he quotes Vivekananda. Karimul fills the void of a real hero in the lives of many.

Though Raju and Rajesh have now taken over the responsibility of the bike ambulance, Karimul still has to supervise and organize other activities that he has undertaken or initiated for the poor. Added to these, almost every day, Karimul has to attend one or two public events. So he decided to be very selective about which events he would attend, but this created an unforeseen problem: the organizers of the events he turned down thought he had become arrogant. Being a noble soul, he does not want to hurt anyone. Thus, he has requested that unless it is absolutely necessary, people should not invite him as a guest or chief guest to their programmes, but his plea has fallen on deaf ears. Despite his unwillingness, he still has to attend many functions and gatherings.

Karimul's name has also cropped up in the Parliament. After receiving the Outstanding Parliamentarian award in August 2018, a senior lawmaker from Bihar, Hukum Narayan Yadav, cited the example of Karimul in his speech. Hukum Narayan said that he had been inspired by Karimul to aspire for the Outstanding Parliamentarian award, despite coming from a humble background. He eulogized the achievements of this tea garden labourer in front of the parliamentarians.

Karimul is a champion for the people of the entire state of West Bengal. His selfless service to the poor, despite being a tea garden labourer, has instilled the belief in many that they, too, can serve the downtrodden, irrespective of their own limitations. Ordinary people can identify themselves with him very easily. A rickshaw-puller in Kamakhyaguri in Alipurduar district celebrates his birthday every year by feeding countless poor people because Karimul is his hero and an inspiration for him.

Yes, Karimul is the poor people's messiah and a role model for the young generation.

Acknowledgements

As I mentioned at the outset, my father, Binay Bhushan Jha, has been my biggest inspiration when it comes to working for others. Another inspiration for me was my soft-spoken but strong mother, Bibha Jha, who ensured that my father could work for the society without worrying about us. Not formally educated, she always encouraged me and my two siblings to study and make it big in life, and change our own fortunes, as well as those of our fellow men forever.

My younger brother, Dr Debajit Jha, now an assistant professor of economics at O.P. Jindal Global University, who is more of a friend to me, has not only been my partner in crime but my companion of dreams for a better day. Sitting in a far-off village in West Bengal, we challenged all our disadvantages: social and economical.

Acknowledgements

We spent many a sleepless night dreaming about our rosy futures. Nothing could stop us from making some big strides despite our struggles. My little sister, Durga, who has also done well in life, has been close to me since a very early age. I would also like to mention the names of Subhadip Mukherjee, Sunetra Ghatak and two little children in our family: Mohor and Rabbi. I was part of a joint family that included my uncles, aunts and cousins (Ritabrata, Debabrata and Sayan), and my younger uncle Biman Jha who died recently and who always encouraged me in whatever I did in life.

As they say, for every bad person there is an angel. My cousin Dr Anirban Pathak (Bhuta Da) came into my life when very few people outside my family supported me. When other relatives tried to create hurdles for us, Bhuta Da stood rock solid with us, guiding us through the difficult times. I also had another cousin, Tanmay Chakraborty (Bappa Da), who helped me at a time when I was struggling to find a way in my life. I owe a lot to Durga Ma (Jethima) for feeding us on the numerous days when our cook used to bunk.

After completing my masters in mass communication in 2005, Bhuta Da asked me to stay with him in New Delhi as I started my career as part of the national media. Without him and his wife, Papia Chowdhuri, I would not have become who I am today. I would also like to mention the names of eminent journalists Krishna Jha, Dhirendra Kumar Jha and Kanchan Gupta who helped me get my first break as a journalist. My first posting was in Bhopal, as a reporter for the *Pioneer* newspaper. It was a completely unknown city and I faced a lot of problems in my initial days. There, three persons—Feroz Mirza, Akbar Khan and Fauzia Bhavi—came to my rescue and never let me feel that I was away from home. I would also like to thank my first resident editor, late Sanjeev Majupuri, and our city editor, Rahul Narhona. But it was Feroz Bhai who protected me from everything I had to face as a young rookie staying far from home.

I came back to Delhi in 2007, thanks to Suvam Pal, who now works as a foreign editor with a news channel in China. My next job was at Zee News, where I worked till I came back to north Bengal in 2013. In Delhi, I met some wonderful people, some at my work place and some outside of it. At Zee News, my boss, Akrita Reyar, played a huge role in shaping my English-writing skills. I also miss my friends Raj Khurana, Deepak Sahu, Vaibhav Arora, Chayan Rastogi, Vineet Ramakrishnan, Feroz Khan, Ajith Vijay Kumar, Shashank Kumar, Prajwal Pariyar, Hemant Abhishek, Suyash Srivastava, Gaurav Raj Thakur, Amlan Chakraborty, Subhankar Mukherjee, Sushanta Das, Pika Jha, Professor Avijit Pathak, Jaydeep Basu and Sudeshna. I would like to express special gratitude to Raj Khurana, who made me feel as if I had never left Delhi, despite having left the city six years back.

I would also like to thank Adaitya Dutta, Sachin Singha, Ganesh Pal, late Sudhamay Dutta, Sukesh Mandol, Subrata Mandol and Karuna Prasad for shaping my nationalist views.

Back in north Bengal, I met some people who always stayed with me irrespective of ups and downs. My childhood friend, Amit Sarkar, deserves special mention. Asim Adhikari, Chayan Bhattacharya, Vijay Shah, Parag Mitra Majumdar, Raju Roy, Sandip Roy, Amar Bhowmik, Biswajit Roy, Saptarshi Nag, Subhankar Roy, Tanmay Goswami, Sahadev Barman, Victoria Rahman, Durba Moitra Chattopadhyay, Chandana Chowdhury, Jayanta Das, Subhashis Munshi, Abhijit Sinha are others I am grateful to. I would also like to mention the names of some of my friends in Cooch Behar: Suparna Nandi, Moumit Dey, Rik, Mum, Debalina, Rhikrita, Shamim, Sangeeta, and all the teachers and staff of Epic Public School, who always encouraged me. I would also like to thank Dr Abhijit Das and Vijay Chandra for always encouraging me.

I would especially like to thank Santanu Jha (Raja Da) for always encouraging me to dream big. Another person who has always stood beside me is Goutam Deb, tourism minister, West Bengal. I would also like to thank Laxmi

Limbu Kaushal, Confederation of India Industry (CII) head, north Bengal and Sikkim, and the entire CII North Bengal team for encouraging me in every venture I have undertaken after quitting my job.

I am also indebted to my English teachers: Manomita Dattagupta, Ranajit Kumar Mandal, Sandip Goon, Kamal Kanti Dey and late Kamal Kanti Bhattarcharya.

For this book, I owe a lot to Mampi Adhikari who first introduced me to Karimul and accompanied me to his house during the course of writing this book.

For the photographs included here, I would like to thank Ripan Biswas, who was awarded Wildlife Photographer of the Year (2019), Sanjay Sarkar and Nirmalendu Chatterjee.

Last but not the least, I would like to mention the names of three people who played a very crucial role in shaping my life in the last decade. My wife, Dr Sanjukta Saha, who has supported every eccentric decision from quitting a high-profile job in New Delhi to running a charitable football academy for the poor children in my native village, Rajganj, has been my biggest strength. Another person is my father-in-law, Dr Sandip Kumar Saha, who has always stood by my side. My lucky mascot, however, has been my handsome and charming son, Shreejit (Zico). It's after his birth that my life started taking a new direction. And it's his presence that fulfils me as a human being.